ISO 9001:2015

ISO 9001:2015

Understand, Implement, Succeed!

Alka Jarvis

Paul Palmes

✦✦ Addison-Wesley

Boston • Columbus • Indianapolis • New York • San Francisco • Amsterdam • Cape Town
Dubai • London • Madrid • Milan • Munich • Paris • Montreal • Toronto • Delhi • Mexico City
São Paulo • Sidney • Hong Kong • Seoul • Singapore • Taipei • Tokyo

For information about buying this title in bulk quantities, or for special sales opportunities (which may include electronic versions; custom cover designs; and content particular to your business, training goals, marketing focus, or branding interests), please contact our corporate sales department at corpsales@pearsoned.com or (800) 382-3419.

For government sales inquiries, please contact governmentsales@pearsoned.com.

For questions about sales outside the U.S., please contact intlcs@pearsoned.com.

Visit us on the Web: informit.com/aw

Library of Congress Control Number: 2016931672

ISBN-13: 978-0-13-452443-6
ISBN-10: 0-13-452443-8

Text printed in the United States on recycled paper at RR Donnelley in North Chelmsford, Massachusetts.
First printing, March 2016

Contents

Preface

In today's environment, the increased competition in the global economy has made it an absolute necessity for businesses to focus on the quality management system (QMS) as a means to increase productivity and create products and services that will yield positive customer experiences. This technique has been proven to guarantee survival in an environment marked by world-class competition and to create excellence, based on a set of philosophies, procedures, and actions that are the hallmarks of a constantly improving organization. The QMS emphasizes application of quantitative approaches, with experienced resources, to improve processes within an organization and exceed customer expectations. Today's businesses widely recognize the need for QMS to assure a disciplined approach to service and product quality, to safeguard customers from related problems, and to shelter the organization from the lawsuits that can arise as a result of inadequate quality.

The technology used by businesses has advanced in the last decade, and the enormous power of social media in shaping the reaction to business brands is widely appreciated. Owners of businesses recognize this power and know that social media can be used as a tool for marketing purposes—but only if the quality of their products and services and the level of customer satisfaction with those products and services are high. Business owners realize they must listen to the voice of the customer and concentrate on quality and defect prevention. At the same time, business proprietors are keenly aware that social media can have a negative impact on their brand if their service or product is deemed unsatisfactory.

The purpose of a QMS is to enable the company to provide a quality product or service to its customers, attain complete customer satisfaction, and gain a larger market share by following key quality management principles and regulatory requirements. Doing it right the first time—and following this philosophy every time—is the most important consideration for a successful business, as this approach will increase productivity and lower costs.

The QMS standard, ISO 9001:2015, is designed to assist product, solution, and service organizations in meeting customer expectations and delivering an overall positive customer experience. ISO 9001:2015 is published by the International Organization for Standardization (ISO), along with other industry-related standards. Adherence to the processes outlined in these standards helps to control problems related to quality and ensures that these issues are addressed at functional levels of an organization, thereby eliminating the potential for a negative impact on customers. The end result, it is hoped, will be profitability and sustainability of the business enterprise.

The authors of this book are seasoned quality assurance professionals. They have been staff members at small and large businesses in various capacities, starting from being members of line operations, to staff management, to executive management, to high-powered consulting. They have successfully implemented quality management systems, performed audits, trained auditors, and have done extensive consulting. They have been involved in the development of ISO 9001:2004 and ISO 9001:2008. They participated in authoring ISO 9001:2015 and ISO 9000:2015 ("Quality Management Systems Fundamentals and Vocabulary"). ISO 9000:2015 supports the vocabulary and terminology of ISO 9001:2015. The content of this book reveals the extensive experience both the authors have in the field of quality, in designing and implementing effective quality systems in various industry sectors.

The purposes of this book are twofold: (1) to provide individuals and organizations with an important tool to understand the newly revised ISO 9001:2015 quality management standard so that they can achieve and maintain excellence, and (2) to promote continual improvement through the implementation of this newly revised standard. The requirements of ISO 9001:2015 are clearly presented in this book as building blocks, with each block defining the value derived from the clauses of the standard. The authors offer a logical, structured process to implement ISO 9001:2015 that will improve quality in your products and services and result in higher customer satisfaction.

If you have already implemented ISO 9001:2008 in your organization, this book provides guidance on the differences between ISO 9001:2008 and the new and revised content of ISO 9001:2015. The discussions of these differences will help you determine the gaps and identify the components needed to bring your existing QMS up to par with the new requirements.

This book does not address statistical quality control or other "total quality management" principles. All of these subjects are extensively addressed by many other books and authors. Instead, this book is an in-depth guide to understanding the revised ISO 9001:2015, which provides detailed explanations to empower you to successfully implement the newly established requirements of this standard.

Throughout the book, the authors have explained each requirement of the standard in simple terms to allow you to comprehend the quality elements involved. Here is a quick guide to the book's contents:

- Chapter 1 highlights the business relevance of ISO 9001 and emphasizes the importance of operational excellence.
- Chapter 2 provides an overview of the call for the ISO 9001:2008 revision, the various activities performed to justify the need, the impact of the changes, and constraints and benefits of the revised structure. The two chapters that follow discuss various opportunities to reevaluate your QMS.
- Many readers may hear that "output matters" and wonder how to interpret this popular cliché. Chapter 3 focuses on the opportunities within ISO 9001:2008,

explaining in detail how to develop a restructuring plan and providing guidance on what it takes to address the concept of "output matters."

- Chapter 4 discusses the components that make a compelling case for leadership to implement effective governance and reviews some of the tools commonly used to achieve compliance. The content of this chapter serves as a foundation for positive results; it is intended to help you understand the needs and expectations of your customers as well as those of interested parties. Without this knowledge, regardless of how hard you try to meet customer expectations, you will fall short.
- Chapter 5 focuses on understanding the organization and its context, determining the scope of the QMS, and understanding the needs and expectations of interested parties.
- Chapter 6 outlines the commitment required from leadership; the role of the quality policy; and the importance of organizational roles, responsibilities, and authorities. The leadership in any organization is the most critical element in determining the success or failure of a QMS. Indeed, by changing the actions of management, the philosophy, values, and behaviors of an entire organization can be altered. Grassroots efforts by line staff are certainly commendable, but without the firm support of leadership, a great idea will never take root and deliver lasting rewards. Robust quality systems require a cultural change, and the reality is that cultural change cannot survive without the constant support and encouragement of top management.
- Chapter 7 highlights the fact that no matter how well you have identified the activities and the requirements of the QMS, without a solid, well-understood, well-communicated plan, efforts to identify risks and opportunities, meet quality objectives, and plan for change will be fruitless.
- Chapter 8 elaborates on the resources, competences, awareness, communication, and documented information needed to support the QMS.
- Chapter 9 discusses operational activities such as planning, control, requirements related to products and services, design and development, control of externally provided processes, product and service provision, and nonconforming products and services.
- Lord Kelvin's quote, "To measure is to know," is a very appropriate epigraph for Chapter 10, which focuses on performance evaluation of the QMS. Such an assessment can be carried out by conducting internal audits, monitoring, measurement, analysis, and other forms of evaluation. An organization cannot begin its transformation until it is aware that the quality of its product or service must be continually monitored and improved. Chapter 10 also addresses management reviews, explaining why they are crucial to the continual improvement of the QMS.

- Chapter 11 discusses nonconformities and the actions that should be taken to analyze true root causes to prevent them from happening again in the future.
- In the concluding chapter, Chapter 12, we highlight further improvement opportunities for business excellence and emphasize the use of ISO standards as a foundation and enabler for improvement.

The appendixes provide a summary of the quality management principles that are the foundational elements for any QMS. They also list other standards relevant to the food, telecommunications, and health care industries, among others. Appendix C provides further details on documentation. Appendix D compiles various templates that can be used as is or customized depending on your needs and the size of your organization. Appendix D also offers salient examples of opening meeting agendas for external audits as well as closing meetings. These examples, along with others, are intended to assist you in understanding some of the topics that should be covered in various audit-related meetings.

In summary, this book is intended to appeal to a broad range of readers, including those who fill the following roles:

- Vice presidents/directors of corporate quality, responsible for an overall company-wide quality management system, including product quality and associated processes
- Managers in charge of TQM, managing and developing strategies for company-wide processes to increase project effectiveness and customer satisfaction
- Directors of operational excellence, responsible for overseeing defect-free, smooth running of all processes related to operations
- Quality engineers (manufacturing, service, hardware, or software), responsible for ensuring quality in their respective day-to-day jobs
- Testers, or those in charge of testing products (software, hardware, firmware), to ensure that they follow pre-established processes according to ISO 9001 requirements
- Software quality assurance managers, responsible for evaluating software quality by designing new development processes to increase the overall quality of their products and provide a positive customer experience
- Process improvement engineers, in charge of benchmarking against world-class organizations, implementing what has worked for other companies, ensuring that processes bring beneficial results, and planning new activities to improve overall product/and or service quality

There are no prerequisites required to read this book. However, you should have an orientation or context based on quality management and an awareness of industry standards for quality and regulatory requirements. Because of our experience, we understand the challenges of those who will end up implementing ISO 9001:2015. Our goal is to provide basic and understandable guidance to implementing ISO

9001:2015 by exploring necessary details and the often simple logic of quality, considering how quality excellence relates to customers, and examining the essential role of senior management.

Acknowledgments

With a book of this breadth, it is almost impossible to acknowledge all those individuals who have made significant contributions to this collective body of knowledge.

Approximately 60-plus worldwide quality experts (including us) from more than 40 countries met regularly in international meetings, over WebEx, and in small teams around the world during the past three years to develop and finalize the contents of ISO 9001:2015. We would especially like to thank them.

Finally, we wish to acknowledge our editor, Kim Boedigheimer, and our production editor, Elizabeth Ryan, and to thank them for their patience and guidance.

About the Authors

Alka Jarvis has 30 years of experience in software engineering, including 19 spent in total quality management. Her background encompasses management of large scale systems/solutions development, product and process quality assurance, IT security, industry standards and regulations, and corporate training.

She has frequently been an invited speaker on quality assurance topics at international as well as domestic events and has worked in a variety of capacities for Fortune 500 companies such as Cisco Systems, Apple, Bank of America, AT&T, and others.

Alka is an adjunct lecturer in computer engineering at Santa Clara University. She is also an instructor for the software quality courses at U.C. Santa Cruz and U.C. Berkeley Extensions. She won Silicon Valley's "Corporate Woman Advocate of the Year" award for her accomplishments in the software quality field. ASQ in Milwaukee, Wisconsin, recognized Alka by publishing her accomplishments in their "Who's Who in Quality" article.

Ms. Jarvis was named as an expert on Industry 4.0/Smart Manufacturing and represents American National Standard's Institute (ANSI)/US, in the strategic advisory group at the international level, to the ISO's Technical Management Board.

In her role as the chair for the past nine years, representing the United States to the Technical Committee 176 for the International Standards Organization (ISO), Alka has been instrumental in the development of ISO 2000, 2004, and 2008 versions of ISO 9001 and 9004 Standards. She was in the drafting committee of the latest 9001-2015 version and is an ISO Lead Auditor, certified by Exemplar Global of United States.

Ms. Jarvis is currently a member of ASQ's Learning Institute Advisory Board; served as the president of the Bay Area Quality Assurance Association (BAQAA); has been an Applied Total Quality Advisory Board member for U.C. Berkeley Extension; an advisory board member to the Certificate Program in Continuous Improvement and Quality Management at U.C. Santa Cruz Extension; board member for Quality Assurance Institute; an advisory member for ASQ's 2015 and 2016 International Conference on Quality Standards; and vice president of the Indian Business and Professional Women network.

Paul Palmes is principal consultant with Business Systems Architects, Inc., of Fargo, North Dakota, and Prescott, Wisconsin. Working as a specialist in quality management and world-class quality systems over the past 27 years, he has enabled many organizations to attain ISO 9001 registration and many others to improve profitability and culture. He is a Certified Quality Manager and a BSI Certified Lead Auditor. He is an active podcaster who educates worldwide listeners through his "Quality 101" program series at http://www.pdcauditing.com. His many publications include two books, *Process-Driven Comprehensive Auditing* and *The Magic of Self-Directed Work Teams*, published by ASQ Quality Press, as well as articles written for ASQ's *Quality Progress* magazine and the *Auditor Newsletter*, published by Paton Press. He is currently chairman of ISO TC 176 SC 1, responsible for the revision of ISO 9000.

1

Quality Management Systems: Adding Business Value

The business case for ISO 9001 begins with its central mission—namely, enhancing world trade. ISO 9001 was developed during the same relative time frame as the European common market. Representatives from throughout the world met during the 1970s and 1980s to determine best business practices and requirements for each such practice to ensure consistent and conforming output of goods and services. The underlying principle was and remains a simple idea: Two companies operating in much the same way can expect equal treatment in managing everything from new orders to customer complaints. Of course, developing such a standard is also a rather ideal undertaking. By their very nature, all standards define an ideal state within which people—and indeed entire societies—work cooperatively, ever mindful of the best interests of all. ISO 9001, by recognizing the ideal state as rarely achievable but nonetheless a worthy aspiration, established the concept of continuous improvement to guide and motivate organizations to advance and succeed.

None of this works if you don't know who you are or where you're going. ISO 9001 therefore requires organizations to analyze their current state of affairs, define and set goals to achieve future expectations, and then monitor progress toward those goals. Top management, which is responsible for defining these goals, is therefore in need of feedback to determine how best to distribute resources. Those departments or processes that are most challenged become candidates for receiving additional resources. ISO 9001 defines all these interrelationships, some of which also require records to prove that decisions were developed and implemented based on facts, not assumptions.

Of course, this is all just "good business." Leaders decide policy and set goals to move the organization forward. Metrics are established to monitor progress. When it becomes clear that metrics are below expectations, additional resources are provided to improve performance. Finally, those same metrics are used to determine the return on investment for those additional resources. Through this activity, the company becomes an improvement engine. Assuming that the marketplace embraced and supported the outcome of all this effort, the obvious result should be sustained success—that is, a win-win scenario for both the organization and its customers.

ISO 9001 is good business on several levels, but perhaps most importantly it offers proof of performance and therefore accountability at all operational levels. Businesses and business leaders are accountable to any number of internal and external demands. A few examples serve to illustrate this point. Shareholders want improved earnings, while the accounting department is clearly correct in submitting a costly requisition for new enterprise resource planning (ERP) software. Customers, though not willing to pay more for it, are increasingly interested in additional software functionality, even though the design team needed to accomplish the upgrade is currently cost-prohibitive. These and similar scenarios are commonplace in today's market. ISO 9001 offers a consistent set of methodologies for managing these kinds of countervailing demands. Of course, once the plan is established, the work must then be done. Performance that meets its goals becomes centermost within the organization. Expectations are defined and progress is monitored. The overall result is a new level of accountability, involvement, and visibility.

Traditional top management oversight is accomplished through analysis of monthly financial statements. If the numbers are good, especially the "bottom line," further action is less important than would be the case if profitability was reported to be under projections. But where, exactly, is the problem? Can financial statements alone provide the right answers? In many respects they can, especially if the question is directed to which losses occurred and where they happened. But financials alone do a relatively poor job of answering why and who was responsible for the loss. At best, they are the starting point for further inquiry. Without high-level objectives and department-level goals to achieve them, and without a clear and compelling vision of the future state, ailing performance often skips wildly, from month to month, from one area of the company to another.

Without mutually agreed, high-level goals, the company is a rudderless ship—and behaves like one. Although the captain may want to achieve maximum speed, the crew can, and often does, cite the weather or excessive sea conditions for poor progress. It is also clear that one function—one type of activity that's controlled by the crew—can rarely make any real difference, given the lack of a deep and solid rudder under the ship. And so it goes, month to month, swaying with each variable breeze and hoping for success. The shipping company's financials simply report that income is down, not that any particular vessel is late to unload its cargo.

ISO 9001 and Innovation

Businesses are rarely static; that is, their products and services are always adapting to a changing marketplace. Competitors are constantly eager to improve their bottom line through any number of advances within your own organization's existing customer base. Innovation is no longer an occasional threat; it is the new constant in business worldwide, announced through the Internet and the general media at the speed of light. Innovation is especially friendly to startups, which are eager to gain a toehold or to catapult their companies to mega-status through one or more new approaches to an existing model. Large firms often fall victim to smaller firms as they become comfortable with established sales volumes and less concerned with their ability to remain profitable. Market innovators often target companies such as these, applying their best designers in the quest to outperform the current players whose research and development (R&D) investments have slackened over the years. It is important to note, however, that such efforts are highly focused and deliberate.

It can't be otherwise. Smaller businesses cannot afford extended R&D projects, cost overruns, and missed launch dates. They are small in number and at the mercy of limited supplies of capital and nervous investors. Time to market is critical not only to protect their ideas, but to stay in business at all. For these nascent organizations to succeed, it becomes crucial to produce. For those individuals working in these companies, risk and reward are high, but they are also the very reason why work is exciting and fun. The atmosphere is charged, and communication is immediate as everyone works to achieve the same outcome.

ISO 9001's approach to innovation lies at the center point between the startup and the established company's approach. Remembering that fearlessness is just one step away from recklessness, ISO 9001's design requirements maintain proven risk mitigation criteria while allowing companies to move in any direction they believe to be appropriate. ISO is not restrictive in regard to innovation, but rather responsible. The key to successful design—to any innovation, for that matter—is to define new product expectations, features, and complexities. These are important to achieve focus and clarity as the work progresses. They keep the design team on track. Once the particulars are understood by the team, it is necessary to research any number of "resulting requirements" such as applicable legal issues, standards, or codes to ensure that the market can adopt the product with the assurance that it is free of any unanticipated shortcomings. Controls are defined to ensure that as the product is developed, several "go/no go" sessions are planned to assess the product's ability to provide its originally intended design features. Once things are close to completion, two types of specialized controls are employed: verification and validation. Verification seeks to determine that what's on the print is what was produced. Validation ascertains whether what was produced actually works in the marketplace. Both considerations are extremely important—and validation is especially critical from the perspective of the consumer. A solid design program is careful to spend time researching and interacting with the market prior to launch, if only to determine whether the color is right and the consumer is not irritated by the soundtrack while waiting for an operator.

The point of this discussion of innovation and ISO 9001 is to emphasize that both the established company and the innovator are equally supported by ISO 9001's design requirements, and that neither is restricted by them. In fact, the startup may need ISO 9001 far more than the established company so that it can avoid the potential for costly omissions in its design. The established company can benefit from ISO 9001's initial design planning requirements to avoid "design creep" and cost overruns. Both types of organizations can use ISO 9001's design requirements to better plan and support their design processes, create new products that are embraced by the marketplace, and avoid excessive risk in the launch of new products and processes for managing their services.

The Business Call for ISO 9001

It was once standard practice for large organizations to help their suppliers develop ever higher levels of sophistication in quality, supplier management, and logistics. Supplier quality engineers (SQEs) were tasked with analyzing the supplier base and offering training and other direct help to targeted suppliers to improve their performance and maintain costs. Today, few offer this kind of support. As the price to do so has increased, specialists have taken the place of many former multitasking operations. In addition, the rise of ISO 9001 acceptance has largely transferred managerial oversight to ISO 9001's third-party auditor. As a result, the majority of ISO 9001–registered companies now also require ISO 9001 registration of their suppliers.

It's far less expensive to require oversight than to provide it.

Small businesses constitute the majority of organizations currently registered for ISO 9001. With more than 1 million registrations currently in place, it's also clear that many of these small organizations are registered because of requirements imposed by their larger customers. The call to be "9001 registered" by these larger clients is primarily driven by the cost of maintaining a large staff of SQEs; many have chosen to instead rely on third-party auditors to ensure compliance and related satisfactory outcomes of the audit process.

For most small businesses, the requirement to register is often perceived as a tax on business. Given that these organizations are currently successful in selling and gaining acceptance of their products, what can ISO 9001 add that isn't already in place? The answer is little more than restating the requirement that all suppliers be registered—the perception of ISO as little more than a tax, an additional fee imposed to remain or become a supplier. Indeed, the majority of registrants did so because they had to, not because they wanted to. In turn, many approach the registration process as a "min-for-max" proposition, spending the least amount possible to gain registration and hoping that the net outcome will not excessively hinder their current practices.

This is especially true in terms of maintaining their ability to be flexible and responsive to their customers. ISO 9001 is often incorrectly perceived as a system that slows down operations with additional forms and paperwork, takes more time to develop concepts into finished products, sets up a new layer of bureaucracy through which many decisions and controls have to undergo new and confusing scrutiny, and simply costs more money than it's worth. None of these assumptions need be true, but all have the ability to become so, especially if the min-for-max approach is utilized. Unfortunately, it is easier and faster to overlay a patina of acceptability and compliance through methods that are favorable to the third-party auditor rather than addressing the improvement needs of the company seeking registration.

The min-for-max approach intensively relies on documentation, forms, and reports to provide evidence of compliance to the standard. It can be, and often is, available as a package of materials requiring some basic editing to indicate relevance to the company and its practices along with appropriate training of a select few who have been charged with developing the program. It also sets in place most of the negative perceptions of ISO 9001 as a tax on business because the goal is tactical (registration as a business requirement) rather than strategic (registration to improve business practices and performance). As a result, the company develops work instructions instead of its workforce, produces reports that satisfy specific clauses within the standard instead of specific needs, and compiles documentation structured to convey permanence and authority instead of clarity and understanding.

The call to register to the standard is strong within the marketplace. Organizations face a choice: Do they undertake study and planning for implementation that first and foremost enables and improves, or do they throw together a string of documented evidence primarily relevant to achieving registration? Even if the initial belief of top management is that ISO 9001 is a tax on business, there is much to recommend in the adage, "If all you have are lemons, make lemonade!" The strategic approach allows the company to ride atop the wave, or at least seize the opportunity to develop a clear path to doing so, while the tactical approach most often leads organizations to become consumed by it. Developing your quality management system, whether it be a new registration or an upgrade from the 2008 revision, is a strategic decision, one that will affect the working lives of everyone in your company.

We believe that there is opportunity in the making. The following chapters were developed to define the reasons, methods, and possible tools to achieve initial registration or upgrade to the 2015 revision of ISO 9001 that add value to your business. The 2015 revision is the culmination of many years of development and worldwide acceptance. Chapter 2 examines that history a bit further and explicates the differences between the 2008 release and the 2015 revision. As you continue reading, keep in mind that the intent of the ISO 9001 standard is to enable best practices, not to restrict them. Even though you may be compelled to register by customer demands, it's infinitely better to adopt the position that the organization was instead given the opportunity to improve.

2

Executive Overview of Changes Within ISO 9001:2015

Among the many significant problems facing the business today are consumer demands for better products and services, increased competition, constant technology changes, and knowledge management. You have no doubt heard the exhortation of "faster, cheaper, and better" often in your work environment and in the world around you. The rapid pace at which the global economy is moving leaves less time to develop quality products and less money to do so than were available in previous decades. Of course, to produce a quality product or service, attention must be given to details where all *i*'s are dotted and all *t*'s are crossed. To do this, you need time, which is a very scarce commodity these days due to the shorter time to market that prevails across most industries. Companies are often willing to sacrifice quality to be first in the market to introduce a new concept, product, or service and thereby gain a larger market share. In turn, employees are frequently asked to cut review times, sacrifice on documentation, and streamline testing procedures. But what really helps in cutting down on costs, emphasizing design and development, and increasing quality? In such situations, a well-grounded quality management system (QMS) with appropriate metrics and trending of customer satisfaction can be a company saver. A QMS is combination of organizational procedures, related policies, resources, and processes, that when performed accurately, produces quality products to meet customer requirements.

The QMS standards are a model of how a business can manage key processes of product or service realization, regardless of the size of the organization or industry. Implementing a QMS can help in numerous areas:

- Improve and increase customer satisfaction
- Increase productivity by establishing repeatable, proven processes

- Increase market share by ensuring consistency of the product or service
- Reduce expensive mistakes
- Be able to systematically approach new markets
- Remain ahead of competitors

The world's largest developer of voluntary international standards is based in Switzerland. Commonly known as the International Organization for Standardization (ISO), it provides vigorous specifications for products and services, facilitating worldwide trade through achieving global consensus on the contents of these standards.

Under ISO, approximately 20,000 international standards for various technologies and businesses have been developed, ranging from health care to food and safety to innovation, among others. Work on these standards is initiated and completed by subject-matter experts who are nominated by their national member bodies. The most popular ISO standard is ISO 9001, Quality Management Systems—Requirements, with more than 1.3 million global certifications issued.

ISO 9000 and ISO 9001 are the key international standards related to quality management systems. ISO 9000 addresses the terminology and vocabulary. ISO 9001 is the only standard that is related to the QMS against which organizations can obtain certifications.

Organizations gain several benefits from obtaining ISO 9001 certification. The key advantage is that such registration distinguishes the organization from its competitors; it is a globally recognized achievement that may lead to acquisition of additional global business.

To ensure that ISO 9001 quality management standards remain relevant to the complex, ever-changing business environment, these standards are revised periodically. The ISO 9000 certification standard has changed over several revisions. Here, we review the history of ISO 9001 and the changes that have been introduced with each revision. Prior to ISO 9001:2015, four different revisions were released. Following is the history of each revision.

- **ISO 9001:1987:** The initial 1987 version was based on UK Standard BS 5750, with three "models" for quality management systems: (1) ISO 9001:1987 Model for quality assurance in design, development, production, installation, and servicing was intended for companies and organizations whose activities included the creation of new products; (2) ISO 9002:1987 Model for quality assurance in production, installation, and servicing had basically the same material as ISO 9001 but without covering the creation of new products; and (3) ISO 9003:1987 Model for quality assurance in final inspection and test covered only the final inspection of the finished product. Depending on its specific needs, an organization selected certification based on one of these three models.

- **ISO 9001:1994:** In 1994, minor revisions were made to the 1987 standard. ISO 9001:1994 emphasized preventive action and continued to require evidence of compliance with documented procedures. This led to companies creating tons of documents, which then became cumbersome to update and audit.
- **ISO 9001:2000:** The 2000 version of the standard had dramatic changes that placed new emphasis on process management. The goal of these changes was to send a clear message that the new revision was about ensuring the quality management process was working and yielded positive results, rather than forcing organizations to develop and maintain a huge amount of documents. It certainly paid less attention to documentation, instead focusing on performance measures. Continual process improvement and trends in customer satisfaction were also identified as key issues.

The 2000 version stressed that management should stop delegating quality functions to junior staff; that is, upper executives were expected to become involved in integrating quality into the business system. The set of eight quality management principles shown in Table 2.1 were introduced as a common foundation:

Table 2.1 *Quality Management Principles*

1.	Customer
2.	Leadership
3.	Involvement of people
4.	Process approach
5.	System approach to management
6.	Continual improvement
7.	Factual approach to management
8.	Mutually beneficial supplier relationships

- **ISO 9001:2008:** This revision contained minor amendments and no new requirements. The 2008 version introduced clarifications to the existing requirements of ISO 9001:2000 and some changes that were intended to improve consistency with ISO 14001:2004, Environment Management Systems requirements.

The ISO 9000 (9000, 9001, and 9004) family of standards is developed by Technical Committee 176 (TC176). There are three subcommittees (SC) under the umbrella of TC176, each with clear responsibilities and a set of published Standards (Figure 2.1).

- **Subcommittee 1 (SC1): Concepts and Terminology:** ISO 9000, which describes fundamentals of quality management systems and specifies the terminology for quality management systems.
- **Subcommittee 2 (SC2): Quality Systems:** ISO 9001 and ISO 9004, as well as standards on quality plans, project management, and configuration management. SC2 also develops support information to assist users in understanding these standards.
- **Subcommittee 3 (SC3):** Supporting Technologies: Provides guidance documents to implement and maintain effective quality management systems.

Figure 2.1 *TC176 and Subcommittees with Published Standards*

Revision Process and Rationale for Structural Changes

It was more than 10 years before any significant changes were made to the ISO QMS standards. During that time span, businesses around the world encountered constant changing needs owing to global market expansion, privacy concerns, outsourcing, acquisitions, and other issues. The past decade has proven to be a "golden age" for technology and innovation, bringing dramatic changes to the way we do business, the way we work, the way we communicate, the way we live, and the way we learn. Can you think of a recent week when you did not use Google? Online banking and cloud services, online collaboration, social networking, mobile access, three-dimensional (3-D) technology, affordable Global Positioning System (GPS) devices, fuel-efficient cars and other innovations have all had dramatic impact on our life. In the face of these myriad changes, for ISO 9001 standards to remain relevant, the requirements had to be revised.

In this section, we'll share some of the details of the process used to determine the extent of changes and the drafting process that produced the current contents of ISO 9001:2015. These activities are not listed in a chronological way and some of the steps are summarized (such as ballots of key documents by members); the goal here is simply to give you an overview of the process and raise awareness of the efforts that went behind the decision-making process for the revision as well as the contents of the latest version.

A systematic review of ISO 9001:2008 was conducted according to pre-established criteria in the ISO directives, and a majority of votes from members then approved a revision/amendment and the adoption of the Annex SL "high-level structure." Annex SL is a new management system format that was developed by ISO and prescribes a high-level structure, identical core text, and common terms and definitions to facilitate implementation and auditing of multiple management systems. It was previously known as ISO Guide 83. Guide 83 provided a base structure and standardized text for management system standards (MSSs). However, the implementers of various MSSs such as ISO 9001, ISO 14001, and ISO 27001 complained that these standards had similar elements, but were organized differently, making it cumbersome and difficult for organizations to implement multiple standards. The contents of Annex SL were architected by the ISO Technical Management Board (TMB).

A justification study (JS) for a revision to ISO 9001:2008 was then developed. It is mandatory for all projects for MSSs or for the revision of existing MSSs to obtain approval of a JS by the ISO Technical Management Board before a project can be started.

In addition, a design specification was developed. The design specification provides guidelines, a strategic intent of the revision, and the scope for the revision process.

A proof of concept was developed by members of a work group by plotting the requirements of ISO 9001:2008 into the new Annex SL format. The purpose of this activity was to test whether the requirements could fit within the proposed high-level structure and its clauses.

A task group was formed to discuss and identify future concepts to be included in the new revision. Over several meetings and intensive work sessions, the group identified several concepts with detailed descriptions deemed appropriate to be included in the future revision. Some of these concepts are listed in Table 2.2.

In addition, ISO/TC176/SC2 identified the need to prepare a worldwide survey of users and potential users to better understand current and future customer needs for the ISO 9000 family of standards. A team was established to conduct the survey, which was web based, available in 11 languages, and sent to a wide variety of sectors. Responses were received from 122 countries, and four generic product categories applicable to ISO 9000:2008 (hardware, software, processed materials, and services) were represented. Along with other usability-related questions, the concepts listed in Table 2.2 were included as a part of the survey. The feedback from the survey was used to set the strategic direction for the future quality management standard. TC176/SC2 member bodies were requested to nominate two "experts" to be members of a Work Group (WG) and participate in the development and drafting of 9001:2015. This Work Group, known as WG 24, met several times over the period of three years to complete the writing process. The meetings were hosted by various member bodies around the globe.

Table 2.2 *Future Concepts*

Financial resources of the organization
Innovation
Integration of risk management
Life-cycle management
Resource management
Self-assessment tool
Strategic planning
Supporting quality tools (Six Sigma Lean, SPC)
Systematic problem solving and learning
Use of technology to develop/implement the requirements of the standard
Use of technology to run your business
Voice of the customer

A new WG23 was also formed, consisting of experts nominated by member bodies to manage external communications related to ISO 9001:2015.

Since the original set of eight quality management principles (QMPs) were developed in the mid-1990s by a small group of individuals who had the necessary expertise and were familiar with the quality teachings and philosophies, an ad hoc group was formed to evaluate the old principles and revise them to meet the changing needs of quality management system. This newly formed ad hoc group worked for a number of months and developed seven new QMPs to replace the original eight principles introduced in ISO 9001:2000. These QMPs, which are listed in Table 2.3, serve as a foundation for any quality management system.

Table 2.3 *Quality Management Principles*

Quality Management Principle (QMP)	Title
QMP 1	Customer focus
QMP 2	Leadership
QMP 3	Engagement of people
QMP 4	Process approach
QMP 5	Improvement
QMP 6	Evidence-based decision making
QMP 7	Relationship management

Understanding Changes: Variance Between ISO 9001:2008 and ISO 9001:2015

For those readers who are familiar with the format of ISO 9001:2008, the biggest change to get used to will be the new structure of Annex SL, which has been introduced to ensure the standard remains relevant and to bring consistency. These changes could have a dramatic impact on your quality management system over the next decade. Once this barrier is overcome, the effects of the changes will differ between organizations, depending on their size, industry sector, and business needs. In the future, every management system standard developed will use a consistent structure and outline—for example, identical text, common terms, and definitions—in accordance with Annex SL. Due to the high-level structure format mandated by Annex SL, the structure and clauses of ISO 9001:2015 have changed as well. Most of the requirements of 2008 are found under a new clause or subclause in 2015.

Companies that have implemented a QMS based on individual clauses and developed their quality manual accordingly may struggle to meet the new standard. Consistent results are obtained when all interdependent processes within an organization work together as a whole system—a concept emphasized in ISO 9001:2015. For example, in a car, the ignition, brakes, engine, and other parts must function together for the car to operate in perfect condition. If one part of the car is nonfunctional, it will have negative effect on the smooth running of the vehicle.

The following information highlights some of the high-level differences contained in ISO 9001:2015 as compared to ISO 9001:2008. Some of them are major, while others are minor and barely noticeable.

- ISO 9001:2015 follows the Annex SL structure, which outlines a common structure for all ISO management standards.
- ISO 9001:2015 has 10 clauses, instead of the eight clauses found in ISO 9001:2008.
- The term "products" is replaced by "products and services" to make the standard applicable for service-oriented organizations as well as those organizations that deal with products.
- The term "exclusion" is not used.
- ISO 9001:2015 introduces a 4.0 clause regarding the context of the organization; it focuses on the organization to determine those external and internal issues that are relevant to the organization's strategic direction and affects the ability of the organization's quality management system to achieve the intended outcome(s).
- Clause 4.2 emphasizes the need for products and services to meet the appropriate regulatory and statutory requirements, along with determining the

interested parties that are relevant to the quality management system and the quality management system–related requirements of these interested parties.

- ISO 9001:2015 focuses on the quality management system and its process approach in clause 4.4, by highlighting key activities such as process inputs and outputs, correlation of processes, resource availability for the processes, and other requirements.
- Clause 5.1.1 requires leadership to be accountable for the effectiveness of the quality management system. This will create a larger need for the leadership to be involved in the successful operation of their QMS.
- Clause 6.1 requires an organization to consider issues referred to in clauses 4.1 and 4.2 when planning for the quality management system; to determine the risks and opportunities related to product conformity; and to achieve results leading to continual improvement.
- Risk management is now an important element of quality and must be extended to "externally provided products or services." For example, outsourcing is subject to risk management; that is, organizations must address risk management in their evaluation of suppliers that are used for outsourcing. To control externally provided products and services, associated processes will require more detailed attention.
- Although risks have to be identified and acted upon, there is no formal requirement for risk management. It is up to each organization to determine its plans to meet the requirements related to risk.
- ISO 9001:2015 emphasizes change management in several clauses, due to the fact that effective change management results in productivity increases, reduces the need to revamp processes, increase revenues, and boosts employee satisfaction.
- A variety of requirements are related to change management. For example:
  - Clause 6.3 explicitly requires the organization to consider the purpose and probable consequences when a need for a change to the quality management system is determined. Lengthy requirements related to planned changes to the management system are introduced, along with consideration of the purpose of change and the availability of resources. These requirements must be understood and any changes required for the effective operation of the QMS must be planned.
  - Clause 7.1.6 requires the organization to consider existing knowledge and evaluate the need to access additional knowledge based on changing customer/business needs and trends. Strategic consideration of talents and knowledge needs is required for the smooth operation of the QMS and to confirm products and services that will result in customer satisfaction.
  - Clause 7.5.3.2 discusses control of changes and gives version control as an example.

- Clause 8.1 emphasizes the need for the organization to control planned changes and review the effects of unintended changes.
- Clause 8.5.6 discusses review and control of changes in production or service provision and requires the organization to retain documentation related to this kind of review.

- Organizational knowledge is specifically called out in clause 7.1.6, where an organization determines required knowledge for the successful operation of its quality management system to ensure conformity of its products and services.
- Clause 7.4 has extended requirements related to communications, including external communication, and is more prescriptive in regard to what, when, with whom, and how to communicate. A clear description of the methodology of communication must be developed and implemented.
- Additional attention must be paid to determination of the extent of post-delivery activities (clause 8.5.5).
- The concept of relevant interested parties is introduced in clauses 4.2 and 4.3. Relevant interested parties are individuals such as customers, competitors, and the organization's various committee members who can impact the organization's capability to supply products and services that meet customer and applicable regulatory requirements. The organization makes decisions about the relevancy of these individuals.
- The use of preventive action is eliminated. Annex SL does not include a clause giving specific requirements for "preventive action," because the key purpose of a robust quality management system is to act as a preventive tool to build products and offer services that are right the first time.
- ISO 9001:2015 refers to documented information rather than documentation, documented procedures, records, and quality manuals, all of which were requirements in the previous version of the standard. The new standard does not require creation of a quality manual or documented procedures, but there are specific references to "documented information" that needs to be retained or maintained. However, to support the operation of the QMS, the new version requires the organization to maintain documented information (documented procedures) and retain documented information (records) necessary to have sufficient confidence that the processes are executed according to plans.

Impact of Changes on Implementation

The fundamental intent of ISO 9001 is to emphasize the requirements for a sound quality management system and thereby instill confidence in the organization's customers and improve their experience with the product or service. The new requirements of ISO 9001:2015 address this need.

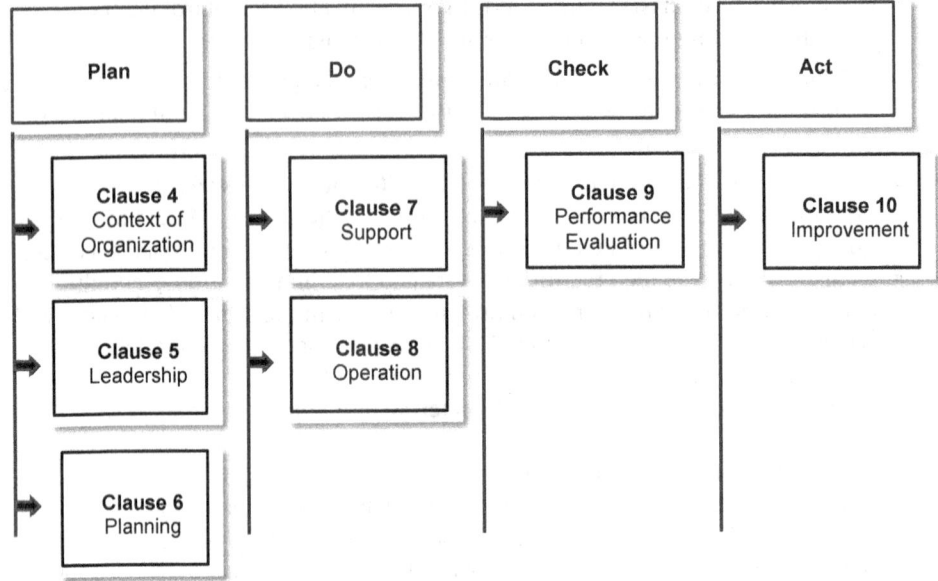

Figure 2.2 *Plan, Do, Check, Act*

For those organizations that strongly believe in Deming's PDCA (plan, do, check and act) concept, Figure 2.2 shows how the clauses of the new version fit together with the PDCA concept. The PDCA concept shown in Figure 2.2 can further be broken down by individual activities that affect the quality management system. Depending on the depth and breadth of your QMS, these activities will differ. However, the overall principle will remain the same. For example:

- In the *plan* phase, you may address:
  - Quality policy
  - Quality objectives
  - Scope of the QMS and its processes
  - Leadership and commitment
  - Roles and responsibilities
  - Needs of the customers
  - Understanding of the organization and its context
  - Planning for changes
  - Identifying risks and opportunities
  - Allocating resources for support
  - Identifying the competence of the individuals performing the work
  - Communication
  - Documented information

- In the *do* phase, you may address:
  - Operation planning and control
  - Determining the requirements for products or services
  - Design and development
  - Controlling outsourced products and services
  - Production and service provision
  - General release
  - Control of nonconformities
- In the *check* phase, you may address:
  - Internal audits
  - Management review
  - Monitoring, measurement analysis
- In the *act* phase, you may address:
  - Nonconformity and corrective actions
  - Continual improvement

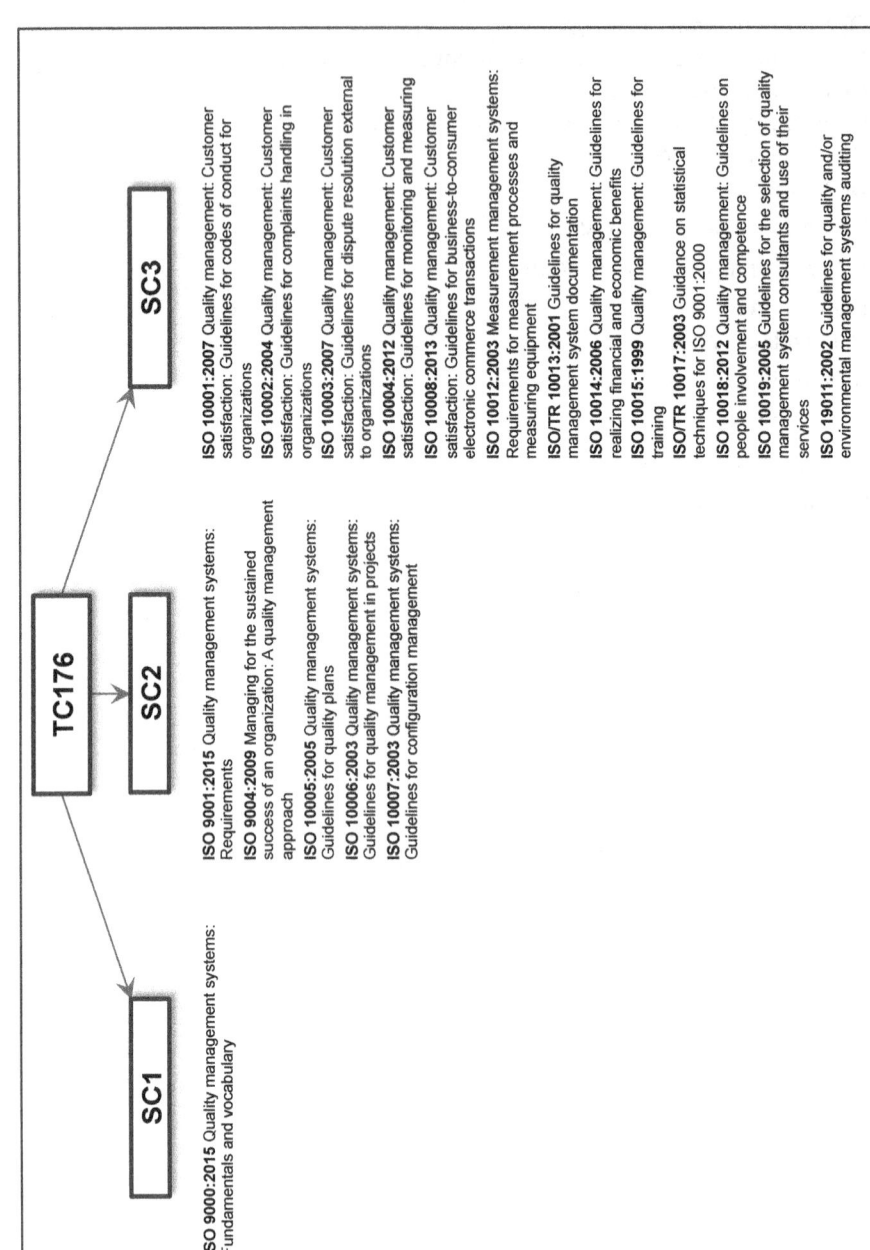

Figure 2.3 *ISO 9001:2015 Clauses and PDCA Concept*

Constraints of the Revised Structure

The need for adequate resources to implement a result-based, meaningful quality management system is often undermined by the leadership of an organization, and adequate knowledgeable, trained resources are not always allocated from the beginning of the quality management effort. We have seen companies where there are a barely adequate number of employees to manage the QMS. For example, one large company with 50,000-plus employees had fewer than 10 individuals assigned to conduct internal audits, provide consultation to various functional organizations in implementing processes, ensure corrective and sustainable processes were put in place where nonconformities were found, and so on. Having the right number of qualified resources available is certainly a key to success when implementing your QMS.

As noted earlier, the ISO 9001 standard forces all new ISO management system standards to adhere to a high-level structure, with a set of common text underlying that structure. If your QMS is built on ISO 9001:2008 individual clauses, it will take strong change management activities to change the culture to view different clauses of ISO 9001:2015 as a whole QMS, where all the clauses work together to deliver optimal results.

Benefits of the Revised Structure

The constraints listed previously can easily be viewed as benefits as well. For example, the high-level structure can also be a benefit if your organization has to implement multiple management standards. ISO 9001:2015, through the Annex SL's format and common structure, can save hundreds of hours and resources in the implementation of multiple management systems standards, thereby increasing productivity.

The 2015 standard was developed by taking into account rapidly changing technology and addresses a few of the latest concepts with positive customer experience and satisfaction in mind. The goal is that the latest standard will remain relevant for a number of years.

ISO 9001:2015provides separate annexes. These give further clarifications, making the requirements of the new standard easy to understand and interpret. The informative annexes are:

- **Annex A** gives clarification on the new structure, terminology, and concepts.
- **Annex B** lists other international standards on quality management and quality management systems developed by ISO/TC176.

A new guidance document, "ISO/TS 9002 Guideline for the Application of ISO 9001," has been developed and is available for purchase. This guide interprets ISO 9001:9015, thereby making it easy for organizations to understand and implement the standard, and to be successful in business while using it. The document also provides clarity to external auditors, leaving little room for interpretation of the requirements.

Transition to ISO 9001:2015

There is a period of three years allowed after the publication of the standard for transitioning to the new version from ISO 9001:2008 (until approximately September 2018). The best method to proceed in adopting this standard will be to first conduct a gap analysis to determine the extent of work involved in transitioning to ISO 9001:2015. Our recommendation is for you to start making your senior management aware of the coming changes and to ensure a transition plan is in place.

3

Opportunities to Reevaluate Your Quality Management System

Value-Added Restructuring of Your Quality Management System

Business thrives on results. Successful businesses, in turn, recognize that results are the outcome of sound planning and well-defined goals. Regular oversight of each major process and those processes' combined success as a system is standard operating procedure for any business owner, vice president, or senior manager. This oversight may be formal or informal, ranging from board room to lunch room meetings, but the intent remains the same. Management, either alone or working with other staff members, develops and embraces a vision against which new challenges emerge throughout the organization. This vision describes the "future state" and is designed to challenge the status quo. Each department assesses its abilities and resources to achieve this future state, or what is often called "the next level."

Evaluating the state of the quality management system (QMS) begins with a frank and open discussion with top management to determine if your vision statement is strong and compelling. Some companies have developed a mission statement instead of a vision statement—either is appropriate. The central question is whether the content of one or the other provides direction and purpose.

A company's vision states what it intends to be. It is a call for the organization to become something better, larger, improved, and so on. Ideally, the vision statement is a one-sentence description of a clear, inspirational, and long-term change. A vision takes work, commitment, and enthusiasm to achieve; it is a call to action. The Internet offers numerous examples of vision statements, just a few of which we offer here:

- **Amazon:** Our vision is to be earth's most customer-centric company, to build a place where people can come to find and discover anything they might want to buy online.
- **Apple:** Apple is committed to bringing the best personal computing experience to students, educators, creative professionals, and consumers around the world through its innovative hardware, software, and Internet offerings.
- **Microsoft:** Create experiences that combine the magic of software with the power of Internet services across a world of devices.

A quality management system—indeed, any management system—must have a reason to carry out its activities. A strong vision provides a common focus for these activities. Nevertheless, many organizations have tended to develop quality management goals that are different from or exist beneath a company's business goals. That is, they often create goals that apply to only one function or department. As your QMS develops, be especially mindful that performance metrics for each process should be easily traceable to your organization's overall vision.

In small businesses, this vision is often as simple as one word: survival. Taking on new challenges is an accepted practice. Small businesses rarely turn down new work—they can't afford to do so. It's standard practice to swing from one type of work to another, taking pride in the company's ability to perform a wide variety of activities for each new project. Even so, these companies operate in much the same manner as large organizations, in that each new opportunity is addressed with a planning session, often involving the entire staff. Staff members discuss the job among themselves; make many of their decisions based on group experience; and develop plans for required materials, new tooling and machinery, and even expected overtime. The new project may be completely different from the last one—but the vision drives everyone forward.

Success leads to a "can-do attitude" that can be both a strength and a weakness. Bidding for work they've never done while still achieving the customer's expectations strengthens everyone's perception that dedication and hard work can overcome any challenge. Planning is well intended, but often misses several important and unknown details that then lead to setbacks and frustration throughout the job. The planning process is usually not documented, nor does it include process failure-mode effects analysis (PFMEA), control plans, or other formal tools to identify potential problems and remedies. Instead, there may be a meeting in which prints are passed around the table and little more than light discussion brings about consensus to proceed with the bid.

The large company compartmentalizes this process; teams of specialists have replaced a small group and perform their work within a vision that is far more defining and succinct. Whereas the small organization strives to survive, the large company is confident in its ability to do so and has defined its special niche in the marketplace. Its vision defines a future state of prosperity and success in this particular type of work, such that the organization rarely wanders into other ventures. Most larger organizations learned this discipline in their early days; that is, they learned what they do best as a collective response to having survived their past.

Throughout the process of growth from a small company to a large enterprise, employees remain vital to the organization's ability to move forward, to implement the activities required to transition from talk and planning into actually doing what is needed to achieve a new tomorrow, to realize the company's vision. The vision must therefore be clear and compelling. To be truly compelling, it must define how to succeed. When people embrace a vision, they become committed to it. Their future success is then linked with the success of their company; their loyalty inspires both themselves and others. While it is true that the days of "lifetime" employment are gone, few would argue that it remains the goal of all employees to find their "perfect job."

Defining the vision, which clarifies for everyone what the company strives to become, is only the first step toward attaining the desired results. Most employees work within their respective departments, each performing different tasks. Because each department contributes something uniquely separate from the next, each must also clearly define its individual contributions to the vision and the means by which it will measure its success. Once these departmental or process goals are defined and measurement criteria established, training programs can be developed to enable employees to perform their work in a manner that will satisfy these departmental goals and thereby collectively contribute to the organization's vision.

Naturally, these departments must also be properly equipped with resources to accomplish their goals. A department will struggle to make its unique contributions to the organization's vision if it lacks the necessary people, tools, and resources. Of course, each time performance is measured and lagging indicators are analyzed, resource restraints are likely to emerge. In that event, management must listen and respond accordingly to retain its credibility. After all, managers own the vision as well as its ramifications, including the constant need to negotiate its cost.

At this point, the company is operating as an engine, improving as a result of monitoring its goals, learning new things, rearranging its resources, and improving its original plans. It has created a feedback loop that provides the necessary fuel to analyze its efforts against its goals and then modify its actions as necessary to achieve the vision. As organizational excellence improves, the desired results will follow. Over time, improvements will also demonstrate that there is value to continuing this work.

Of course, the most significant measure of success in terms of the organization's achievement of its vision is a positive marketplace reaction. Such significance may be direct or indirect, hidden but still noticed by the customer. It could be as simple as a logo that elicits a smile, a reputation for honesty, or a unique business setting. Internal improvements may, for example, minimize price increases, provide outlets with replacement inventory more efficiently, or refine packaging in a manner that is noticed and appreciated by the consumer. Other improvements are more obvious, making it easier to measure the customer's reaction. Opening an outlet in a previously subserviced location, overcoming a known product shortcoming, or decreasing prices by virtue of greatly improved internal efficiencies can be measured in terms of both testimonials and an improved bottom line.

Customers are the ultimate judge of success. They are the most significant beneficiary of an organization's output. Organizations whose quality systems clearly establish and communicate goals to achieve their vision and develop improvements incorporating the voice of the customer have captured the essence of a quality system.

Customers' voice is vital, perhaps even more so than the "internal numbers." After all, if they don't buy the organization's products, there's no reason to make them. Many try, but few companies do well in this area. The consumer is a difficult-to-fathom creature—one that is hard to understand, other than by calculating how many are buying the product. But when they stop buying, how will the company know what to do without a strong flow of good information from its customers? By themselves, sales figures are a positive indicator of customer satisfaction—at least until the moment sales decline. Clearly, that's too late to step in.

To maintain business value, companies need both internal performance data and customers' external response data. Both are the raw materials for improvement, the fuel needed to drive and maintain business value.

The essence of a successful business system can be summarized as follows:

- Establish a clear vision.
- Communicate the vision throughout the company.
- In support of the vision, develop performance measurement criteria for important processes.
- Establish and implement performance reporting methods and frequency.
- Establish and implement customer satisfaction reporting methods and frequency.
- Provide new guidance or resources for lagging performance.

Each of these elements is represented in Figure 3.1, a self-assessment form found at the end of this chapter that was designed to start the conversation about value-added restructuring and continuous improvement in your company. The narrative here was intended to awaken thoughts of restructuring, especially for those who have been ISO 9001 registered for many years. As you work through the restructuring process, keep in mind that many other forces are at play and that rethinking is paramount to building an improved approach.

Focus on Competence versus Paperwork

In the early days of ISO 9001, the standard relied on a simple, but misguided construct that assumed process documentation and extensive records would produce a consistent, conforming product. Time and experience have proved otherwise, so much so that the 2015 revision of ISO 9001 requires no documentation at all. ISO 9001:2015 leaves the decision of what must be documented, to the organization, with the aim of not imposing a requirement where a company's size and complexity may not warrant one or more documented descriptions of what everyone already knows. The need for records continues to be recognized in the 2015 revision, but there is a distinct difference between an important, on-file purchase order and dust-laden purchasing process documentation, especially in a small purchasing department. Records are required to prove a past activity; documentation is required when an activity cannot be successfully performed without it.

The best example of required documentation is the preflight checklist. No airplane, commercial or private, can begin its roll down the runway without the pilot taking the time to review and confirm each item is operating within the established parameters. The order in which each item is addressed has been carefully determined to build a cascading "if-then" series of verifications, building one atop the other to determine airworthiness. It's easy to understand the importance of faithfully checking off each item—some were added in reaction to a previous disaster. Each item on the checklist documents an activity (air flight) that cannot be successfully performed without it. If the completed checklist is retained electronically (as most are nowadays), it becomes a record.

Another example of required documentation was witnessed by one of the authors while auditing a remanufacturing company specializing in the teardown and repair of large tractor transmissions. The process required that service manuals and specialized work instructions be made available to operators whose jobs required that they safely remove nuts and bolts, gaskets, and cover plates in a very precise order, often using specialized tools and fixtures. One operator made it clear that variations in the received transmissions and the amount of time that might pass between calls to work on a particular model made it impossible to remember everything without these manuals and work instructions, even though he was a 12-year veteran. As this example illustrates, the activity (disassembly) cannot be successfully performed without these documents.

Competence

Of course, the 12-year veteran has a distinct advantage and higher status compared to any new employee. Indeed, his or her experience is often considered priceless. As an experienced employee, this individual now uses documentation more as a reference, though it once required careful study and application. Such an employee has completed the first, and perhaps second and third, readings, and now has the ability to refresh his understanding rather than concentrate on each word or diagram. The involved veteran employee can also be considered a competent employee, assuming years of training, concentrated study, skills, and experience.

ISO 9001:2015 continues to emphasize competence as opposed to paperwork. The preflight checklist and disassembly work instructions mentioned earlier are members of a small club of activities that cannot be successfully performed without documentation. Actually flying the plane requires innate and required skills learned and applied under the watchful eyes of an instructor. Likewise, the disassembly process requires a senior worker or supervisor to guide the employee through the basics and other special techniques to succeed in the job. Both of these activities require a mentor, and both are highly particular processes, requiring some level of documentation to succeed. However, most work can successfully be performed with only the most basic documentation. Competence is heavily weighted toward repetition and mentorship. In this process, a new task is explained and demonstrated by a trusted coworker; the employee observes and then performs the required activity. Many such training sessions are actually hampered by existing documentation, as it is all too frequently outdated and/or poorly written. The act of learning, of becoming competent, requires concentration, instruction, and repetition to know the process sufficiently to perform it correctly. In ISO 9001:2015, mentorship is defined as "sharing undocumented knowledge and experience."

The 2015 revision of ISO 9001 also requires records of training, as has been the case since the inception of the original standard. Your QMS will require a method to capture a mentor's assessment of training, often recording the start and end dates of the mentorship; the end date signifies acceptable performance by the trainee and the employee's ability to successfully work independently of others.

Most work fits into this scenario. It follows logically that whenever possible, paperwork and unnecessary documentation are to be avoided in favor of mentorship to achieve employee competence. A positive result matters more than the paperwork it took to achieve that result. Unnecessary records and work instructions are no longer considered to anyone's advantage; that is, ISO 9001:2015 is written to promote competence, not paperwork. If, as most companies, your organization primarily relies on "sharing undocumented knowledge and experience" as the basis for developing competence, you need to examine the leftover clutter in your system from previous compliance requirements, both real and imagined.

Paperwork

Paperwork is never mentioned positively. We've never overheard coworkers praising paperwork as their favorite activity—quite the contrary. Of course, when they criticize paperwork, they're really expressing their dislike for the waste associated with *unnecessary* paperwork—that is, the time devoted to filing, organizing, analyzing, and managing data and information instead of doing other things they believe to be more important: "I want to be the service manager, but all I seem to be able to do is manage a ton of paperwork with little or no time to help my staff." ISO 9001:2015 does not require any specific documentation or excessive record keeping. Those who take the position that ISO 9001 is paperwork intensive are maintaining a myth based on older revisions of the standard. It certainly doesn't have to be this way. Even if the solution is to transfer unnecessary paperwork to a clerical activity, any solution is far better than perpetuating the paperwork myth and wasting the talents of competent people by turning them into clerks. Legacy documentation and unnecessary record keeping can be eliminated throughout your system. After all, if it doesn't add value, why continue to maintain it? If it doesn't drive the company to improve, why are you using it?

The 2000 revision of ISO 9001 began the transition of moving away from the mindset that "to document is to control." The process of documenting is often quite valuable, however. Bringing together all interested parties to discuss process flow and particulars does create a deeper understanding of how things work; many times it leads to several improvements as well. In such a case, it is actually the process of documenting—not the document itself—that holds the most value. The document will age as the business changes and employees come and go within the system. Revisions become afterthoughts without enforced, formal oversight. Documentation maintenance by a few is far less rewarding than the initial process of developing and brainstorming among a connected group of people. In time, the bulk of an organization's documentation becomes a rarely used resource, there for auditors to unearth as compliance guides and to pinpoint a key phrase or operation that was disregarded in the event of a nonconformance. Even so, it is all paperwork and primarily a compliance activity.

If your organization is "drowning in paperwork," that scenario is not the result of instituting ISO 9001:2015. Rather, it is the organization itself that has imposed the need to send reports, attend unnecessary meetings, and generate process documentation and work instructions. Of course, there will always be a need for employees to meet, produce records, and create documentation, but that need is no longer driven by ISO 9001, because the standard no longer requires these actions and activities.

The primary driver for QMS paperwork is usually regulations handed down by your customers. Customers typically want copies of your quality manual, your audit schedule, and any number of documents they believe to be necessary for process controls and product integrity. The same can be said for product safety regulations and inspectors. They may require documentation that is not required by ISO 9001:2015, but is necessary just the same. Your QMS will therefore be populated with three types of documentation:

- Documents your company believes to be necessary for the QMS
- Documents your customers believe to be necessary for their oversight and control
- Documents required by statutory and regulatory concerns

One last example of rethinking before we move on to another topic: The 2015 revision of ISO 9001 no longer differentiates between documents and records. Both are now referred to as "documented information." Our use of the older descriptions is still valid, however, as Annex A.1 notes that the terminology used in the documentation of an organization's quality management system is simply a matter of choice. You can choose to use terms that suit your organization's operations rather than those within the standard. This is a very meaningful concession to the working world and the words we use to express ourselves. If "goals" are more acceptable than "objectives" within the normal speech of your organization, then "goals" should be used.

Customer Expectations and Quality Certifications

It has become commonplace to see flags, signs, and banners posted against businesses proclaiming that they are "ISO 9001 Certified." Technically, they are ISO 9001 *Registered*, having received a certificate of registration from their registrar. Regardless, those who have worked to successfully register to the standard are rightly proud to advertise their accomplishment. Those who drive by the facilities proclaiming that accomplishment are usually impressed, as the ISO brand still garners considerable respect throughout the world. As of this writing, as mentioned in Chapter 2, more than 1.3 million companies have successfully registered their operations by a third-party auditor as compliant with ISO 9001.

Of course, those companies have not registered their *products* as compliant with the standard. Rather, their registration is in relation to their *quality management system*: the people, processes, and content of those processes observed by their registrar as compliant with the requirements of ISO 9001. In other words, the registered organization has been observed as doing the things that are important to do to produce consistent, conforming products. Its methods are registered, not its products. That's why buildings may carry ISO 9001 signs, but products do not. A tire manufacturer may be ISO 9001 registered, but the tires cannot carry an "ISO 9001

Approved" sticker. The company may say that the tire was produced in an ISO 9001–registered facility, but no more.

Some who recognize the brand are less impressed. They once thought that an ISO 9001–registered company would naturally be capable of supplying them with acceptable products, only to be disappointed by the quality or delivery of that company's goods and/or services. They took care to investigate the supplier's capabilities beforehand, requiring a self-survey, a copy of the company's ISO 9001 certificate, and a short audit of the supplier's facility. Yet, when it came time to perform, the supplier was obviously less than capable of meeting most requirements. Worse, its response to several nonconformances indicated that its approach to corrective action was entirely unacceptable.

A registered organization might underperform for any of several reasons. For example, the company may be a new registrant, just getting started in the process. It may have all the necessary documents and records, it may have trained the staff as best it could, and its registrar's auditor may have recommended the organization for registration based on adequate, though limited evidence of compliance.

It's also possible that the registrar's auditor may have been lax in his or her oversight of the company and not probed deeply enough into nonconformance or corrective action records. If an auditor is unaware of concerns lodged by the organization's customers, especially complaints and nonconformance responses, a meaningful, accurate assessment of the organization cannot be expected.

In some cases, both the supplier and the registrar's auditor may have grown too comfortable with the relationship. Over time, the audit function may have become secondary to maintaining friendships while irregularities are brushed under the carpet with smiles and assurances that the condition is temporary and will resolve itself soon. What should be a major nonconformance might be written up by the auditor as an area of concern. A progressive registrar will enforce a change of auditors to counteract this sort of complacency every three or so years—a practice we strongly advocate.

There are still more potential explanations for an underperforming but still ISO 9001–registered organization. Auditing is a hard job. It's written into every closing meeting that the process cannot be expected to investigate everything within a QMS; that is, an audit is just a sampling of the system. Key individuals within a company and its QMS may come and go, replaced at times with persons less capable or still grappling with its complexities. The bottom line is that any relationship, especially the choice of a new supplier, should recognize that the ISO banner is secondary to a vigilant investigation of the company's full capabilities. This includes the possibility of a mock exercise to test the strength of a prospective supplier's corrective action process or enforcing probationary status until it is proven that regardless of the supplier's ISO 9001 registration, all systems are in sync with your company's expectations.

Remember, your company will likely be challenged at some point by a customer that claims your own goods or services are not performing as expected. As you reevaluate your QMS, spend valuable time probing your corrective action process, especially the strength of customer communication and root-cause analysis. Perform the same tests when selecting new suppliers. Customers are increasingly requiring their suppliers to be registered to ISO 9001 and other management system standards. Many expect that registration will naturally equate to product excellence, and the majority of registered companies live up to that expectation. Unfortunately, we also know that mistakes will happen. Thus the true test of a quality management system is its ability to manage "quality spills." It's not about the banners or the framed certificate in the lobby; they are only the first step in a continuously evolving improvement plan. The primary expectation that your organization should apply when evaluating a prospective supplier registered to ISO 9001 is that only time and experience will prove if its systems meet your company's needs.

Operational Excellence: The Process Approach

The most significant quality advance in the past 100 years is the computer. These devices are able to capture, store, and analyze data to generate actionable information; they provide for unparalleled machine operation and consistency, and support far-reaching measurement and control. Any discussion of operational excellence must credit the computer and accompanying software as the foundation of current and future advances. Spreadsheets can collect massive amounts of data and compress it into a series of graphs or control charts that display process capabilities and machine performance; they are the tool of choice. A management system also relies on the everyday and occasionally inventive use of computers to help it identify any number of concerns. To fulfill this goal, however, the QMS must measure important, relevant data. It must use a software system that complements its needs and is capable of monitoring all important processes. The bigger picture is that a quality management system is itself a type of computer. That is, the QMS gathers input, processes it through any number of filters and applications, and then distributes information to enable decisions.

Software in this context is a metaphor for any and all tools the QMS uses to monitor the current state, because just as computers capture and organize data, so too does a well-structured quality management system. Lagging machine or other operational performance issues are identified through computer output just as a QMS uses its corrective action or nonconformance database to identify process issues and lagging performance. The interconnections within the QMS act as sensors to discover and promote analysis of potential underperformance. The opportunity to reevaluate your QMS therefore includes development of an effective "process approach."

Operational excellence begins with the identification of important QMS processes and their expected performance, or output. Call centers need to know average wait times and other key metrics to gauge their ability to meet varying customer demands, for instance, just as production facilities require metrics to gauge machine downtime and employee utilization. Even so, the call center and the production floor represent only one process within an overall system of processes in the larger organization. They may well be the most important process and therefore subject to the most intense scrutiny, but they cannot perform to their highest potential without the support of other processes. Purchasing, design, engineering, warehouse, and human resource processes, for example, have the power to either enable or disable these primary processes, yet it is common practice to blindly accept their performance or to assign metrics whose overall value is nearly meaningless to these "support" processes. Purchasing is not as rigidly measured as the production floor when the metrics used are simply procedural. To claim that purchasing metrics measure supplier performance (a necessary component of the ISO 9001 standard) is far less effective than reporting the percentage of supplier improvement obtained through purchasing employees' efforts. Human resources personnel may claim to hire and complete initial training of new employees against a goal of less than x days, but what is even more important is the metric of retention of these same new employees. It is far better to set a goal for reducing employee turnover, as this factor has a larger impact on the organization as a whole.

Design departments, for their part, are besieged with time-to-market demands. The market doesn't reward delay, and the first company to introduce a new product or service is lauded for its inventiveness and insight. Meeting the launch target is as important as any other design requirement, but not the most important. For example, thorough validation is essential to ensuring user acceptance and satisfaction. Less than adequate validation leads to the opposite condition, including potentially expensive warranty claims.

Operational excellence is the product of an enterprise-wide evaluation of the appropriateness of the organization's existing metrics and an examination of other possible or in-place process metrics. The goal is for each process to regularly report its performance against meaningful criteria. When the organization is operating in this manner, important issues become evident sooner and nonconformance is not strictly confined to the traditional celebrity processes of on-time delivery, zero quality spills, and similar concerns. (Yes, in highly focused organizations, an inventory adjustment for a missing part may also a nonconformance!) Underperformance is noticed, bottlenecks readily identified, and the interconnections between departments ever more recognized. The process approach recognizes that the input to one process is most often the output of its predecessor. It further recognizes that transforming an input into an output must be carefully planned, and that each output (the result of that transformation) must be properly measured and monitored. The application of the process approach can be transformative, as accountability is spread throughout the company and quality becomes everyone's concern—both as the sum of the system and within each process itself.

Operational Excellence: Enabling Business and Innovation

The final installment when considering opportunities to reevaluate your company's application of ISO 9001 asks whether your application of the standard enables or restricts growth and innovation. One international registrar requires its auditors to address this simple but very important question as their final consideration during every ISO 9001 audit. As mentioned earlier, too much paperwork restricts innovation and growth, projecting control as paramount and demanding obedience of all involved. This may be quite appropriate for a nuclear power plant, but not for Apple's design department. Call center operators are more effective when they focus on solving a customer's problem in real time rather than writing extensive call summaries.

A requirement must not be fulfilled through blind obedience. It's true that employee training is required to be documented, but it's not true that documented training must be extensive and time consuming. Most importantly, the requirement to document training must make sense to those who record the event and those who subsequently use those records. For example, how can a supervisor know who can rightly be assigned to a particular process or work center in a large organization without a training matrix or other record of training? Employee performance reviews also use training records as a primary input. The record stands as evidence that assigned training from the last review has been completed. Also, because most organizations use performance reviews as the basis for pay increases, the relevance and importance of training records eventually make sense to everyone.

In small companies, where "everyone knows everyone else," it's more difficult to justify maintaining these very same training records. Don't forget—the majority of ISO 9001 registrants are small businesses. Small organizations have fewer training aids, checklists, and work instructions, but ISO 9001 is blind to size. However, we stand firm in stating that a requirement must not be fulfilled through blind obedience. The small business must maintain records of training, but where is the return on this investment that makes sense to everyone?

Records of training are first and foremost a record of accomplishment, and it is basic human nature to take pride in achieving something, be it tangible or intangible. When we accomplish something tangible, the product of our labor represents a statement of skill, growth, and maturity. Intangibles are not visible unless applied in some manner; consequently, they are more difficult to quantify. The training record, therefore, is the only tangible proof of all the work, concentration, and sacrifice it took to develop a new set of skills designed to benefit not only the employee, but also his or her coworkers and the company as a whole.

For these records to have greater significance, they must become tangible. While it's easy to check off and date an employee's training status in a spreadsheet, the individual can't actually hold the result of that step in his or her hands. Moreover, while a printed, single-sheet training log may be tangible proof of an accomplishment, it's not something that inspires pride in posting what is little more than a template. Instead, the organization would be well advised to create something that can be a proud point of reference for these accomplishments. One small company we've visited placed a white erase board in the hallway between the front office and the shop floor. Each of four work teams was represented by large columns containing the names of its employees. Beside each person's name was a space with a dozen small boxes representing the 12 training sessions required to become a "certified operator." As each employee progressed through these 12 training sessions, (what the company called the "core curriculum"), a medallion was placed within the appropriate box. This approach was highly successful, as both individuals and teams silently competed to prepare their members to learn and progress through the core curriculum. Employees found greater acceptance from fellow workers and took pride in applying themselves to training in large part due to that tightly grouped set of medallions transforming what was once a private record into a public accomplishment. The same dynamic is evident in the case of an office worker—perhaps even you—whose cubicle is decorated with one or more training certificates. Those certificates have significance to you and are displayed proudly; you rightly want to take credit for your accomplishment. In contrast, the rank-and-file production workers usually do not have a single workplace or work center capable of allocating sufficient space to post their training records.

The erase board example is only one of several ideas your company might consider as it reevaluates its approach to not just training records, but all records. The goal is to maintain flexibility and enable employees to contribute to the success of the QMS through meaningful activities, not simply paperwork and maintenance. Records of management review (ISO 9001:2015, clause 9.3) need not be long and detailed accounts of who said what. In fact, a dated agenda would suffice, along with action items. The goal is to not overproduce and to find at least some value within the requirement. Those organizations that adopt the opposite approach and build (or have built) mountains of documentation and records typically reduce their flexibility and innovation in proportion to those efforts.

There is no requirement in ISO 9001:2015 to build a bureaucratic and bloated system of approvals, documentation, and records. The standard makes clear that documentation depends on the size of organization; the type of activities, processes, products, and services it creates; and the complexity of those processes and their interactions. The competence of people is the last consideration in clause 7.5.1 that might determine how much the organization should document. Unless you are registering to ISO 9001:2015 for the first time, however, it is not only possible, but almost certain that your QMS is a candidate for eliminating unnecessary documentation. The standards writers in WG24, the working group that develops revisions to the ISO 9001 standard, have been advocating results instead of documents; there are no longer any procedures that are required to be documented, and neither must there be a quality manual or a management representative. Of course, your customers might ask that you retain some of these elements, but after their concerns are managed your organization must take a long, hard look at its approach to documentation in relation to flexibility, growth, and innovation.

A business that loses its ability to innovate falls behind its competitors that foster this talent. Ideally, all ideas—both good and not so good—will be brought to the attention of decision makers as fuel to move the organization forward. The not so good ideas are not discarded, but rather "parked," in the event that they might attach to and thereby benefit a future idea. There is not a single gatekeeper minding the flow of ideas and communication, nor are there several assistant gatekeepers whose ultimate place in the organization is to support the primary gatekeeper's rules and requirements. Instead, the rules are few but clearly stated, and people are rewarded for what they do and not who they are. The 2015 revision of ISO 9001 introduces the concept of risk-based thinking, along with the explanation that when properly applied it becomes less necessary to be prescriptive when requirements are monitored against performance-based metrics. In other words, if your company practices reasonable risk assessment and containment by assigning performance metrics to a process, it's less important to document how the process was designed to perform: "It's all there for the eye to see." Innovation is about change, novelty, and originality that must become a working reality to be effective.

Developing a Restructuring Plan: Who, How, and Focusing on "Output Matters!"

If some or all of the preceding discussion inspires you or your company to recognize that restructuring your QMS is a good idea, the odds are that you will find ISO 9001:2015 to be your new best friend. First, the 2015 revision contains a completely new clause numbering scheme. Second, several of those clauses are new to the standard. Restructuring "because of these new requirements" offers a convenient way to fend off the natural pushback to which any new practice or activity is subject. We call it "the power of a third-party demand." Of course, ISO 9001:2015 clearly states that there is no requirement to renumber or otherwise physically restructure your existing documentation, but few will dispute that it promotes clarity and eliminates a language that requires reference to potentially both old and new clause numbers. Again, the call to restructure can be beneficial. It's not required, but it offers a fresh start from which many companies could benefit.

Restructuring also offers a new opportunity to train employees. Analyze current nonconformance and corrective actions, including warranty issues. Add in customer satisfaction and profitability—the list of topics to be addressed by training is potentially endless, but the result is the same: You can develop a clear picture from these sources that allows you to concentrate on what's missing in your training program.

Restructuring presents the opportunity to transform both the organization and its employees. Companies eventually recognize that all the initial effort to become registered was directed toward installing a host of often missing records and requirements. A new language had to be added to operations that included such phrases as "analysis of data," "management review," and "realization of product." People were trained to work with new procedures and templates. All these activities brought about a single objective of attaining registration, but not necessarily sustained excellence and a culture of continuous improvement. The latter achievements are transformative in nature. Registration is just the beginning, the first level of establishing a system capable of engaging in transformative activities.

Nevertheless, there comes a time when top managers recognize that a truly effective QMS must serve the company first and the standard second in those areas where activities have been put in place solely for the purpose of passing the next surveillance audit. The internal audit program is just one example where too often audits are performed because they're required. Nothing can be further from the truth. While ISO 9001 requires that an audit program be a "planned event," nothing says that an annual audit calendar must be generated. We see these calendars everywhere because most organizations assume them to be required. A planned event can be a monthly or quarterly event, too. The standard goes on to say that audits should be based on "need and importance," the subject of the audit should be that component of the QMS found to be most ailing. Thus, instead of audits for audit's sake, an effective audit program takes into account top management concerns, nonconformance data, and any other QMS input to determine what to audit at whatever interval the company has chosen. The audit program is transformed to become a tool that enables the company to improve, instead of a meddlesome process that no one enjoys or expects to regularly achieve meaningful results.

While it should go without saying, restructuring must be explained in terms that everyone can understand. Moreover, once a path forward has been selected, it falls on top management to publicly endorse planned improvements. "WIFM" is an acronym for "what's in it for me"—a standard component of any sales pitch—and it's no different when explaining a new focus or plan of action for the QMS. People have to know that if they plan, train, and work within the restructured QMS, the end result will be of benefit to them. It has to be clear that one or more specific benefits will directly affect them as a result of their efforts, rather than offering up a vague promise that the company will somehow improve. We also suggest that your company seriously consider sharing with everyone the fruits of restructuring improvements in a way that adds something to the pocketbook. We work in large measure to be paid, and fewer incentives are as strong in overcoming pushback and resistance. After all, you are expecting a return on this investment, so sharing a portion of the expected profit is a win-win proposition.

The restructuring plan can be quite simple. Start with the expected results and work backward to determine which tools and activities are needed to achieve them. For each future result, consult the appropriate clause within ISO 9001:2015 and ask if what you are doing today actually benefits the company or simply maintains your registration. If it's the latter, stop and regroup, because compliance alone carries little value. Work with a small group to convert today's compliance activities into future results that will benefit your company.

With the results and expected benefits clearly articulated, create a plan of action that starts with the lowest-hanging fruit to quickly develop the first successes. Tackle the hard stuff later, once you've built a foundation of these successes. Planning leads to a posted schedule, updated regularly, and to progress reported at every appropriate meeting or gathering. Celebrate successes with lunches, trophies, T-shirts, caps, and whatever else you can provide that publicly represents an accomplishment. These artifacts live on within the company and become a source of pride to each recipient. Pride is a worthy outcome of restructuring and creates momentum. Based on success, pride in your accomplishments establishes trust in the ability to do more and to contribute more effectively, and removes old oppositions to change.

The ISO 9001 standard has undergone three major restructurings since its inception. It's your turn to do the same within your organization by defining a new set of results to transform your QMS into a business management system whose output is quality.

Self-Assessment Form

Present the self-assessment form in Figure 3.1 to your management (or department) team several days in advance of a formal meeting to review everyone's answers and begin the move to a process-based, continually improving organization. The lowest average score becomes the first item to analyze and improve. Similarly, the second lowest score becomes the next candidate for improvement. Revisit and reuse this format as the program matures to continue identifying areas in need of improvement.

Please grade your responses on a scale of 1 to 10, where 10 is "world class" and 1 represents "no activity."

	Score
Does our company have a clear and compelling vision of its future?	
Does everyone in this company understand our vision?	
Have we developed three or four measureable objectives that support this vision?	
Are these objectives understood by the employees of each department?	
Has each department developed its own objectives, goals, and related metrics to ensure improvement?	
Are these goals appropriate to achieving the vision?	
Is the status of each department's goals presented to management on a regular basis?	
Does management provide adequate, meaningful feedback and resources to improve lagging performance to goals?	
Has the overall success of this system been noticed by all employees?	
Have these internal efforts been noticed in a positive manner by our customers?	

Figure 3.1 *Self-Assessment Form*

4

Making a Compelling Case for Leadership and Governance

An organized and well-structured approach to quality is a necessity; quality departments perform important work by carrying out numerous risk mitigation activities within their traditional responsibilities of compliance, cost containment, and improvement. However, in the traditional, compliance-based model, the QMS doesn't encroach upon top managers' daily lives—and in many respects, quality activities are designed to ensure that things remain that way. In the compliance-based model, top managers are aware of many quality concerns but have delegated everything (except their disappointment when things go wrong) to the quality department, which is expected to initiate investigations and corrective actions. Clause 5, "Leadership," and particularly clause 5.1.1 break new ground in the relationship between top managers and the QMS, making it clear that the adage "No news is good news" no longer applies; that is, top management is now required to get involved in quality to a much greater extent than before.

The Compliance Model

The term "min for max" is shorthand for investing the minimum to achieve the maximum. While the introduction to the ISO 9001 standard states clearly that it should be a strategic top management decision to adopt a formal QMS, most companies became or will become ISO 9001 registered simply because one or more of their customers required them to do so. The largest percentage of ISO 9001–registered companies have therefore developed their QMS less as a strategic consideration, and more so as a tactical response to a specific market demand: A customer is demanding it. In addition, if the initially perceived value of a company's QMS is primarily something that must be done to retain existing sales, a min-for-max strategy is quite understandable. Why spend precious funds on—let alone plan for and staff—a system that transforms a company when simple compliance will suffice? With this mindset, registering to ISO 9001 is viewed as akin to paying taxes: You have to do it.

Compliance is an interesting state of being. When an entity is compliant, there's no guarantee, or even a reasonable inference, that it automatically becomes one or more other things. It may not be effective. It may not be profitable. It may not be rewarding, inspiring, or interesting, but it can be compliant. Furthermore, because the ISO 9001 standard is designed to be generic, it contains few hard-and-fast implementation requirements. With unlimited possibilities in how to implement the standard, companies are left to decide for themselves how deeply to invest in each requirement. As a result, and even taking into account that a minimal level of effectiveness must be demonstrated to the third-party auditor, the depth and rigor of a QMS remain subject to interpretation, and are ultimately often guided by that same min-for-max mindset. Compliance is a base-level condition, a state of being that suggests little other than itself. In large part because ISO auditors can award only a passing grade (no C or F or A+ grades allowed during registration or surveillance audits), there is no established incentive for excellence. That must come from the organization itself!

Compliance is—or was—the goal of the vast majority of registered companies when they first applied for registration. Compliance is what everyone works so hard to achieve, once again driven by the demands of one or more current customers. But compliance alone, while certainly indicative of a planned improvement effort, remains a distant second-place finisher to a strategically planned and implemented quality program designed from the beginning to benefit the company first and foremost. The development of ISO 9001, as explored earlier in this book, also offers a lesson in the minimalist outcome of compliance. While the 2015 revision now requires succinct compliance to 11 mostly new requirements regarding leadership of top managers in clause 5.1.1, it does so to counteract the previous compliance-based failings noted with earlier ISO 9001 revisions.

Essentially, compliance was the hallmark of ISO 9001's introduction in the late 1980s. Companies were expected to show compliance in developing more than 20 documented processes and a close number of records of those same processes to serve as proof of compliance. The next revision in 1994 didn't do much to change things. The standard was heavily weighted toward a compliance mindset best explained as the belief that if a process is documented according to stated requirements, the expected results will follow. Unfortunately, while many good things did result from planning and documentation, those same activities became an end unto themselves, creating paperwork and bureaucratic behaviors less likely to improve the company and more likely to drive employees to become unwanted gatekeepers and protectors of their own turf. The concept that documentation produces excellence and the corollary belief that without documentation an audit is severely impaired were rooted in nothing other than the convenience of objective evidence. After all, it's far easier to call up a document than it is to interview and observe. Of course, having a document is no guarantee that people are following its directives, let alone are aware the document exists. The convenience of objective evidence invites yes-or-no responses to audit questions instead of a deep process inspection to determine if inputs and outputs are well managed and expected results achieved.

The writers of the standard knew that compliance was just one factor within a functioning QMS; they recognized that effectiveness is its twin, that both together are needed to forge a truly winning combination. They also knew that a major rewrite was needed to move away from the compliance mindset. Consequently, they spent the bulk of the mid- to late 1990s engrossed in what became the 2000 revision of ISO 9001. The result was remarkable. Only six processes were required to be documented—three representing significant controls, and the remainder important sources of information and activities designed to enable improvement. Also new to the 2000 revision was attention to Deming's plan, do, check, act (PDCA) approach to continuous improvement, and to the notion that effectiveness should be determined and measured in every important process. The problem was (and remains to this day) that while companies were accepting of these changes, most were unwilling to part with the no longer required documentation and other developed controls. Most egregious is the no longer appropriate practice of internal audits that are based on compliance to clauses. The 2000 revision introduced the "process approach," based in part on PDCA, to upgrade the approach to internal audits. Such audits begin by examining process inputs and follow the work to its conclusion, or output. Along the way, resources and controls are examined, as are the people who perform work affecting product quality. The result was designed to be a much improved audit program and one that examines both compliance and effectiveness.

ISO 9001:2015 essentially ends the compliance-based QMS primarily as the result of a single, but profound shift: There are no requirements to document processes. Yes, there are records requirements, now referred to as "documented information," and no one expects that the venerable quality manual will be retired from the language of quality management. Even so, the reliance on documentation to somehow confirm operational control is no longer in vogue. The yes-or-no answer to a compliance-based audit is no longer possible when documentation no longer serves as the basis of the question. This is an important evolutionary tale, and one that the general market and many top managers need to understand, because in this instance the past has not strangled the future. The emphasis on combining the organization's business goals and those of the QMS, the removal of the documentation requirements, and the new requirements to define the context of a company's operations and to really, truly develop an active and effective partnership between quality and top management are all new and, to many, long-awaited changes. In short, the 2015 revision of ISO 9001 is in itself a compelling call for excellence in management and governance.

Paradigm shift, anyone? As you read through this book, remember that though we speak of requirements in ISO 9001, we are not referring to documentation. As you grapple with how to fulfill the intent of one or more clauses, be mindful that it's enough to simply be doing what's required. As a result, audits must rely more on interviews, records, and observation instead of simply looking for documentation. Training can be based on mentorship, not work instructions. Process methods and details can be defined verbally and repeated to the extent that individuals become skilled in similar methods. The min-for-max, compliance-based QMS relying on the ease of documented evidence has evolved into a quality management standard that expects results, not documentation. Top management can expect to be far more involved, as the organization's business goals now are also those of the QMS. In addition, basic compliance can no longer outweigh results when those same top managers are required to actively participate in several important new requirements demonstrating not only leadership, but also the functional end of the min-for-max, compliance-based QMS.

Cost Avoidance

Cost avoidance recognizes that without careful planning, current costs will increase over time. Put another way, without a cost-avoidance program, it will be more costly to operate the business in the future. Quality programs are an excellent platform for cost avoidance, as improvement is at the core of their efforts. The ISO 9001 standard is filled with requirements designed to curtail spending, beginning with a careful examination of the company's place in the world (the context of the organization), followed by an application of its energies to meet the various needs of its most important shareholders. Understanding those involved with your company is key to knowing how to best meet their needs. Here is where cost avoidance can be factored in from the beginning of the relationship: If you know exactly what your customer wants, you can tailor your activities to meet those needs and not others that are extraneous to the customer's satisfaction. A client that wants only parts meeting all its specifications on the expected date need not receive them in elaborate packaging. Of course, this is more an example of elimination of unnecessary costs and not true cost avoidance, but knowing what your customer truly wants to a strong degree sets the stage for a relationship based on the most elemental issues at a reasonable starting price. Cost avoidance, in other words, "begins at the beginning."

Setting the base price is the first step in maintaining the customer relationship and your company's margins. Maintaining that price is the essence of cost avoidance, as supplier costs and the cost of labor invariably increase over time. The first defense to these cost increases comprises reductions in internal waste and throughput improvements, often beginning with the challenge of overcoming the natural learning curve attendant to all new ventures or projects. The organization's QMS is ideally suited to analyze and develop any number of improvements, as its central calling is to capture, analyze, and improve operational methods so as to ensure delivery of a consistent, conforming product. A primary tool for both analyzing the current state and setting goals for cost avoidance is the establishment of key performance indicators (KPIs) in areas critical to maintaining and/or reducing costs.

Key Performance Indicators

Key performance indicators are a window into what an organization believes to be the most important issues it must manage on a daily basis. Think of them as vital business metrics. Like a budget, KPIs provide direction and intent, as each calls attention to those issues and activities that receive primary support. Cost avoidance most directly presents itself in the purchasing realm when key performance indicators are established for supplier performance, quality, cost, and other related metrics. Maintaining current costs and/or working with suppliers to less expensively purchase raw materials is a common KPI, often reported to top management as an annual cost-reduction goal. KPIs are already in place in most service and manufacturing companies, though they may not be formally identified as such. However, when a call center tracks average time on hold or a manufacturer carefully monitors scrap, each metric is, in fact, a KPI.

ISO 9001 requires the establishment of objectives in clause 6.2.1. Careful examination of this requirement indicates that a company's objectives can instead be simply called KPIs. Objectives and KPIs can (and often are) one and the same. After all, objectives are expected to be measurable, monitored, communicated throughout the company, relevant to improving customer satisfaction, and revised when appropriate. Cost avoidance, containment, and reduction efforts are perfect candidates for clause 6.2.1. In the process, clause 7.3 is directly communicated and elevated when factoring in its requirement that those working in the QMS must be aware of these objectives. If your company consistently posts, reviews, and sets goals to meet or beat its KPIs, you are regularly and directly communicating them to those people. Through repetition, employees learn what is important and can relate what they do to one or more of these KPIs. This process is a powerful tool, and when your KPIs are consistent with your business objectives, the QMS is essentially deputizing everyone in the company to act in its best interests. By extension, as top management develops these objectives (KPIs) to ensure the company's success, and if everyone in the company becomes clearly involved, those same top managers will have established a culture that is willing to address and overcome their most urgent concerns.

A Last Word on Cost

Avoiding unnecessary costs is first-order work within a sound and successful business. Those who cannot work within a budget, seldom deliver their promised output, or chronically "invest" in unnecessary upgrades and electronics are operating as if they are above the organization. They are not. In fact, if these practices continue, they may well find themselves not just above, but outside the company—looking for other work.

This admonition is not intended as a business lecture, but rather as an insight into the pitfalls of excessive attention to managing costs. Those who cannot work within a budget or seldom deliver their promised output may also be starved for the appropriate resources needed for success. Their investments in upgrades and other electronics may be seen by top management as unnecessary or excessive, yet they just might require more time to mature. It may also be necessary to stay close to a consumer base that is rapidly upgrading its equipment and approach to utilization. In other words, all costs are not created equal. In addition, while one department's costs may appear excessive, it may be that people were initially asked to do more with less and found the task to be impossible.

Too often missing in this scenario is a commensurate lack of top management involvement. Leadership entails more than simply developing quality objectives, mission statements, and policy statements. Excellent leaders are involved, watchful, helpful, and ready to coach. They are mindful of costs in relation to outcomes, and they recognize that all outcomes are not the product of planning alone. You just can't plan for everything. Yes, implementation is delegated to directors and department managers, as those personnel are tasked with performing the day-to-day activities necessary to achieve expected results. But top managers cannot expect their people to instill the urgency and dedication they know is needed to accomplish the original plan. For those within the organization to fully understand their unique perspective, top managers must publicly set the highest example and encourage everyone, by their own words, to strive for excellence and thereby gain the maximum results from every dollar. Cost avoidance is in everyone's best interests, especially as top management expresses its dedication to these efforts.

Return on Investment

With this section, we have arrived at mission central. Return on investment (ROI) is at the heart of every business decision and is the first term bantered about in every boardroom when considering what to buy and how to address the proposed benefits of that purchase. We have all made a significant purchase, be it a house, a car, or another big-ticket item that required a large outlay of limited cash for something we want or need. Planning for this purchase followed consideration of a highly predictable and rather simple set of questions:

- Can we afford this?
- If we buy it, what will it do for us?
- After we buy it, how long will it take before we realize that it's doing what we hoped it would?

If we actually decide to buy the item, these three questions are followed by a fourth: Did this purchase really bring about the expected results? The same questions must be answered by anyone approaching top management for any and all funding requests. Investopedia.com defines *pro forma* as "a Latin term meaning 'for the sake of form.' In the investing world, it describes a method of calculating financial results to emphasize either current or projected figures." Those within the QMS must recognize that the language of top management includes terms such as these and that few are as significant as pro forma. It is pro forma to recognize that any new project must be presented to top management as the cost to plan, resource, and implement (investment) against the expected increase in profitability (return).

A planned improvement such as the installation of an automated coordinate measuring machine (CMM) must provide something other than the opportunity to perform more interesting measurements. Those measurements might also significantly reduce customer returns, speed up the development of new products, and facilitate other targeted improvements. As an example, let's imagine that returns are indeed flooding the company. Because each return material authorization (RMA) is logged along with its attendant costs, it can be relatively straightforward to engage in a pro forma analysis to determine the total costs of such customer returns to date. If these returns could have been avoided through application of the automated measuring system, and if the CMM were applied to all critical, RMA-related dimensions to stop these returns, the net savings can be calculated once machine installation and training are factored into the equation. This solution is not presented to top management as a possibility or a hunch. The language is not peppered with references to dimensional instability theory, parts per million (PPM) or parts per billion (PPB) calculations, or famous quotations from Crosby or Deming. Rather, the language is direct and focuses on money saved as a result of an obviously necessary investment. In other words, a compelling case for leadership begins with you and your ability to engage top managers on their terms. Do the pro forma calculation of the ROI. We can best engage top management when we emulate their behaviors and concerns, and when we speak the same language that they do.

Developing or maintaining an ISO 9001 QMS is also most certainly an investment—one that must create or sustain a reasonable return. We describe two basic approaches to connecting management's "investment" and quality's "return" later, but need to gently elaborate first regarding what is often called real versus imaginary or soft savings.

Real returns are directly measurable in dollars saved or earned. Monies saved by working with suppliers to reduce the cost of materials and by applying Lean techniques that directly reduce cycle time or decrease required staffing can be measured directly. By comparison, projected savings are harder to prove: An operator suggests an alternative methodology. It's implemented because it's obviously a good idea and several quickly claim that it will save the company a certain amount of money over the next 12 months. That conjecture just might be true, but it is almost impossible to measure. Because this soft or imaginary saving to the company can only be estimated, it will never have the gravitas of a real, recordable reduction in operations. Real or hard savings are noticeable on the bottom line, with a one-to-one increase in profit occurring as the result of an action. Over time, a soft saving often becomes noticeable, but unfortunately additional soft improvements may be implemented during the same time frame and never reported, not the least of which are the positive results of improved employee competence. These additional savings muddy the waters to the point where cause and effect cannot be determined. Moreover, when you add in the multitude of possible additional costs during the same time frame, chances of pinning down the return on that employee's suggestion are nil.

Given this reality, we urge the reader to build the pro forma case based on hard figures. We fully recognize that soft, "intangible" returns are at times the only available metric, but because they are not reflected on the balance sheet, the best advice we can offer is "Use them with caution" if your intention is to truly partner with top management.

Tools, Techniques, and Strategies for Obtaining Management Buy-In

The following tools have a long history of success in connecting elements of the QMS with the concepts and concerns most familiar to top management. Foundational to each is linkage to the actual cost of your QMS program and/or those nonconformances it locates and manages. Each tool has its place. One may be more appropriate than another to your organization or require less effort or money to implement, but enhanced requirements for top management's involvement in clause 5, "Leadership," of ISO 9001:2015 will likely be aided by use of these tools to drive acceptance and implementation. Such tools are also a call for cross-disciplinary cooperation, most notably between cost accounting and quality professionals. The degree of depth may vary from one organization to another, but the use of these tools remains central to effective improvement efforts that involve top management.

Culture is first expressed through its language. On the one hand, the Eskimo tells us of her environment using far more words describing snow than an equatorial native who has most likely never encountered cold weather. On the other hand, that same warm-weather resident has a plethora of terms he uses to express the ocean's condition that are simply not part of the Eskimo's language. To her, the ocean is solid—a sheet of ice.

Top managers' chief concerns—that is, their daily work and value to an organization—revolve around investment and opportunity. The quality professional's day is also consumed by the same concerns, albeit within a different context. Her details, the tools she uses, the issues she faces, and the meetings she attends each day are primarily protective, whereas the top manager's contributions are essentially proactive. Each analyzes data to make decisions. In the case of the top manager, a decision may be related to what was spent or remains to be invested. For the quality professional, a decision may be related to improvement that either contains or reduces costs. One advances the enterprise, while the other enables and protects that advancement.

Traditionally, both speak a different language. Often, the common language of top managers and quality managers is wholly devoid of terms common to each—as if they live in different environments, different cultures. The top manager is as immersed in "ROI" and "COGS" (cost of goods sold) as the quality manager is concerned about "PPB" and "Kaizen."

Figure 4.1 depicts these two worlds and shows the obvious advantage of developing a common set of tools to connect them and their similar activities, though with different perspectives. Not surprisingly, this common set of tools shares a traditional business focus—a primary emphasis on money issues. In many respects, money is at the core of top management decision making. Call it resources, capital, or some other name, but money and the proper management of available funds is the primary concern of top management.

Figure 4.1 *The Overlapping Concerns of Top Managers and Quality Managers*

Cost of (Poor) Quality

The cost of poor quality, often represented as the acronym "CO(p)Q," is a valuable bridge between the world of quality and top management, as it attempts to assign hard costs to waste. CO(p)Q identifies all "wasteful" activities in the organization as one of just four types:

- Prevention
- Appraisal
- Internal failure
- External failure

Most companies are already tracking the costs associated with such issues as manufacturing waste and rework, even if it's just a casual assessment. These additional costs are tangible; a dumpster filled with partially completed parts that were determined to be beyond salvage is a typical example of internal failure. The costs of these unusable parts may be reported in several ways, starting with the price of the new material required to once again start the work. In addition, several costs are at play in this equation:

- The cost of the operator's labor (and benefits!) to initially produce the unacceptable products
- The "lost" cost of machine time and maintaining the heat or air conditioning and the lighting needed to produce the unacceptable products
- Other costs that may arise, such as disruption to schedules, expedited shipping costs and possible loss of "customer goodwill" in the event of a late shipment, and the time needed to manage nonconformance and/or corrective action

Internal waste, in other words, encompasses far more than just the price of additional material! The same is true of each of the four types of waste, but internal failure is most often noticed and measured by organizations because it impacts the material inventory. Inventory, of course, is a line item in most top management financial statements and, therefore, a logical link to the operations side of the company. Once again, the additional inventory needed to produce replacement parts may be noticed, but those other additional costs often remain buried in the overall cost of goods sold (another line item in the financials!).

The same is true for the other three types of waste: prevention, appraisal, and external failure. This brief explanation of CO(p)Q is not intended to serve as a complete implementation guide, but rather as an introduction—one that invites the reader to explore the concept and possibly adopt this tool in your company to bridge the gap between top management and quality personnel. CO(p)Q activities are measured in dollars, a language that top managers well understand. Let's explore the three remaining types of waste to develop a more complete picture of this powerful tool.

If everything worked perfectly, there would be no waste. The scrapped parts owing to the internal failure, for example, were never supposed to happen; the system was developed to avoid just this sort of thing. CO(p)Q begins with this understanding—that if everything worked as planned, there would be no waste. In other words, there would be perfect quality. The organization invests in prevention and appraisal, but once everything is running perfectly there is no longer any need to pay for these activities because, at least theoretically, they become unnecessary.

Prevention activities include training and developing work instructions, procedures, and other tools deemed necessary to educate and maintain process control, communication, and understanding. The same is true for the cost of provided tools, jigs, fixtures, RMA forms, and telephone and computer systems and programs. All of these tools and activities are applied to prevent problems in the day-to-day operation of your business, and each costs money (e.g., the cost to train, the cost to build a new fixture, the cost to add another computer station). Just as each carries an obvious cost, so it also carries underlying costs such as the cost of training a worker, and in the process losing that person's productivity for that portion of the day as well as the productivity of her trainer. By the way, if you are employed as a quality director, the bulk of your salary is likely a prevention cost—and so is the time spent in every meeting you attend!

Appraisal costs are those incurred in checking, inspecting, auditing, and otherwise ensuring that things are operating as planned. If you imagine a typical supervisor's day, the bulk of his time is often devoted to oversight or appraisal activities. Internal and external audits are also appraisal costs, as is the time required for an operator to fill in one or more inspection sheets for produced materials.

External failure costs are the result of escaped internal failures: "Never should've left the building." The worst part of external failure, or customer-related nonconformance, is that it is the most expensive type of waste and has the greatest impact on the relationship between your organization and its customer. No wonder external failure can be very expensive! Tracking the cost of external failure often includes accounting for returned and replacement products, site visits (including airfare, lodging, meals, and other travel expenses), and any number of expenses that have no bearing whatsoever on your actual products. The loss of goodwill is the most difficult to calculate, but may have the greatest impact on the survivability of your company.

Of course, these brief explanations merely skim the surface of CO(p)Q. To really do justice to this tool, it is highly advisable to consult with your finance department, create a team approach to cost identification, and decide how the results will be reported on a monthly basis. "Seeing" these four wastes as sections of a pie chart each month is an amazing experience because it finally answers the age-old question, "What is the real cost of doing business?" Analysis can indicate where and how much money is typically wasted and where to invest (prevention or appraisal) to stem the loss of what should be increased company profits. And here is where this tool excels—because when everything is in place, top managers and quality managers can actually quantify opportunities to improve profitability. After all, every dollar saved through CO(p)Q goes to the bottom line. Research this valuable tool online or invest in any number of books on the subject for further, more detailed implementation advice and direction.

One last word regarding CO(p)Q: As the program develops and true costs are uncovered, most organizations quickly realize that for every dollar in sales, the real cost of poor quality is between 20 and 25 cents. In other words, for every dollar of sales, a quarter is waste!

Corrective Action and Nonconformance Costs

Corrective action and nonconformance (CA/NC) are two additional opportunities to track costs and thereby open lines of communication to and engage your company's leaders, but the cost component must be installed to do so. Because most CA/NC incidents are embedded in the internal failure quadrant of CO(p)Q, adding the cost component may be the perfect place to begin the development of a full CO(p)Q program. For those not yet accounting for the cost of CA/NC, it's not too difficult to establish basic costs for materials, average workers' hourly rates, and average cost of the time required to open the CA/NC and manage the issue to resolution.

These steps are a good start. Of course, if one of the goals in starting the program is to encourage top management to become involved, tracking internal waste is an obvious subject of interest to them. Their monthly financial statements include an element called cost of goods sold (COGS), and a component of COGS is internal waste. Unfortunately, there is usually paltry information in those same financials regarding the real source of that waste. CA/NC, with their associated costs, provide top management with a new window into what and often why profits might be above or below expectations.

Another important element of top management's involvement in CA/NC is their presence in CA/NC meetings. Most quality professionals already know where this is leading. They simply need to look back at previous CA/NC meetings to remember one or two staff members who chronically lagged behind in their responsibilities to close CA/NC and the helplessness of their efforts to push things forward. If top management is present in these meetings, accountability becomes a major factor for everyone. After all, to a top manager, CA/NC is essentially a self-inflicted loss of profitability, whereas far too many workers relate to managing CA/NC details as simply a job that needs tending. Bringing the "profit motive" into the equation by including top managers in the CA/NC effort brings an important perspective to these activities, one that should have been recognized as a primary driver from the beginning.

As a final note, there is an excellent ISO standard that contains many more references to tools that can and should bring top management closer to quality. ISO 10014, Quality Management—Guidelines for Realizing Financial and Economic Benefits, is highly recommended as a starting point when choosing which tool or approach may be best for your company to begin linking top management more closely to your QMS and the bottom line.

Balanced Scorecard

ISO 10014, Quality Management—Guidelines for Realizing Financial and Economic Benefits, might be best described as a management tool box, filled with both financial and quality tools. And the most often cited tool is the balanced scorecard (BSC). The balanced scorecard cannot be adequately addressed in the few remaining pages of this chapter, but the reader will be handily rewarded within any web search for additional materials. The original work was published in 1996 by Robert Kaplan and David Norton in their book *The Balanced Scorecard*,[1] and a flood of subsequent books, articles, and technical journal entries on this topic followed. There is good reason for the popularity of BSC, because it provides a strong sense of focus to those companies that have embraced it to help them both run and improve the organization. For those making the case for top management leadership and governance relative to the 2015 revision of ISO 9001, the use of BSC to frame ISO 9001:2015 most certainly provides a compelling rationale, especially in its application to clause 9.3.1, "Management Review," and a host of other clauses. Management review has several direct components, notably the requirement to assess the adequacy of resources to maintain the QMS, the need to address process performance, the ability of the organization's products and services to meet expectations, and any internal or external changes that could affect the company. The balanced scorecard is a natural fit to monitor these and many other requirements within ISO 9001:2015.

Kaplan and Norton essentially divided a company's efforts and concerns into four component types. Our simplified category titles include finance, product, process, and training.

A company begins by asking itself, "What must I produce in sales to both survive and profit?" (finance). Once the profitability figure is determined, the organization then asks, "Which type of product must I offer the marketplace to achieve this revenue?" (product). This product may require one or more new features to spur sales or a completely new set of offerings. Perhaps sales efforts need to expand into new markets or territories. Regardless, the answer to this question leads to the next, in which the company now asks, "Given the new sales needs, which processes or process improvements will be necessary to produce these products?" (process). Finally, once the process changes and improvements are determined and ready, the company must communicate these changes to the workers (training).

This system is elegant because it can be understood and appreciated by everyone, especially top managers who have most likely studied BSC in the past. Application of BSC to your organization is a parallel effort to ISO compliance, as many of its components are closely equivalent to ISO 9001:2015's clauses and concepts. ISO's objectives are BSC's KPIs. In addition, the student of BSC notices quickly that the system links everyone together at all levels of the company, creating a line of sight from their daily work to the top-level objectives.

We have tried to make a compelling case for leadership and governance by making clear that the old ISO 9001 is gone. Top managers need to know that whatever experiences they may have had in the past, the 2015 revision deserves a second look. The evolution from compliance to results explored earlier in the chapter is especially worth repeating to those managers who have been disappointed in ISO's

---

[1] *The Balanced Scorecard: Translating Strategy into Action.* Copyright 1996 by the President and Fellows of Harvard College, Robert S. Kaplan and David P. Norton, W. W. Norton and Company.

"documented past." Furthermore, while a path to the boardroom is now a requirement, we have offered several finance-based tools that can enable and inform both the quality professional and the top manager as they work together in the planning and implementation of their QMS. Leadership and governance are embedded in as well as aided by ISO 9001:2015.

5

Clause 4: Context of the Organization

We live inside an ecosystem, a place defined by all of our previous decisions and a host of societal forces, past and present. What we do with the available resources and those who recognize the results of our actions also have a decided impact on our present and future efforts. We succeed or fail in this context, and when threatened, adapt accordingly. Context—that is, our background, circumstances, environment, and perspective—requires definition to establish a baseline from which either to continue at the present rate or to grow.

Clause 4.1: Understanding the Organization and Its Context

Reason

W. Edwards Deming is credited with saying, "If you can't describe what you're doing as a process, you don't know what you're doing." He recognized that activities performed without a defined process produce less than satisfactory results. Any number of unintended consequences can and often do compound and confound the outputs of random or disconnected activities.

By extension, the combined activities of a company to create and market its collective outputs, or products, must also be understood as operating within a greater process—that of the marketplace, along with all its attendant forces. If you can't describe the greater process, that of the marketplace, then you also don't know what you're doing. To be successful, companies must both know what they do best and recognize the greater market, or "context" in which these products either gain acceptance or go unnoticed.

Clause 4 was developed to systematically build your QMS atop a full understanding of its context. In plain language, the four steps to building a QMS are as follows:

- What do we bring to the marketplace? (Context)
- Who are affected by our company and what do they want? (Interested Parties)
- Knowing this, what should we be doing—or not doing? (Scope)
- How can we build a system to manage these things? (Quality Management System)

Implementation Guidelines

Clause 4.1 asks your company to look deeply into those internal and external forces that either inhibit or support the ability to achieve your purpose—defined as your reason to be in business, your purpose. At its highest level, this is your organization's stated mission or vision. Analysis of purpose exposes and clarifies many of the internal forces that created the company and have since shaped its internal operations. Purpose is also strategic, in that its components are long lasting and designed to serve the company over the long haul.

The purpose of a company can be most anything:

- Provide employment
- Create a legacy
- Build a business to sell to the next owner or a larger company
- Create and sell a new or unique product

Internal analysis also should expose those things your company does well. Companies that "live their purpose" are focused and seldom stray from their primary strengths. Similarly, internal analysis should expose those projects or products in regard to which your company doesn't perform particularly well. Everyone remembers one or more broken promises and bouts of customer dissatisfaction as a result of overreach and misplaced confidence. Those are learning opportunities and worthy of remembering in the future, because knowing what not to do also focuses a company's efforts toward accomplishing its purpose.

Strategic forces are far more numerous and can apply to both internal and external forces. For example, suppose a machine shop decides to invest in a multi-axis mill to upgrade its current machine capabilities. The new mill will speed production of long-run parts and automate much of the current labor required to make several of these products. Part profitability is expected to rise by 18 percent, and the machine's efficiency allows the owner to bid to make a higher number of complex parts for his biggest customer. Internally, the mill represents a strategic decision to grow the business and retain valued employees, whose work is now less tiresome and monotonous. Externally, the mill represents an important statement to the shop's customers, which now recognize its commitment to long-term investment. The strategic perspective includes recognition and analysis of the following factors:

- Technology and its potential future impact
- Legal issues, including compliance to applicable standards and regulations
- Competition, especially direct competitors
- The market:
  - Current conditions and expected sales
  - Penetration: present and future efforts to gain market share
  - Environmental issues affecting market players
- The economy:
  - Analysis of the local economy
  - Overall economic forces affecting the company, including national and international issues.

All of these "forces" either can or currently do have an effect on the ability of the QMS to achieve its goals.

SWOT Analysis

Consider using SWOT analysis, a methodology that is all but standard practice within the sales and marketing community, because the result of SWOT analysis defines the context of your organization. SWOT is an acronym standing for "strengths, weaknesses, opportunities, threats." A SWOT analysis must include a cross-functional group to incorporate as many perspectives as possible. The reader is urged to research SWOT analysis to achieve a deeper understanding of both its concepts and implementation; however, the following narrative is offered to demonstrate the approach.

Suppose your company manufactures a small, noninvasive medical device that was the first of its kind when it was introduced to the market five years ago. This device is not hard to make; your company essentially assembles eight subcomponents, seals the case, and packages the final product. You were approached by a giant medical device manufacturer (Jensen) last year, which was obviously interested in buying the company, but your founder and CEO turned this suitor down. Word on the street is that Jensen is reverse-engineering your product once again, trying to shrink both its size and its weight by combining your eight subassemblies into a single assembly that is ready to case, test, and ship. Your customers are fiercely loyal, having lived through the dark days before your product was introduced. Your founder's genius has changed the lives of untold thousands of people. Without any direct competition, you essentially own the market. With all of your company's success, you still employ only a small number of people—a continuing source of pride among all employees.

SWOT analysis considers all of these factors, separating each issue or topic and placing it into one or more SWOT categories. It is not uncommon that an identified strength may also be a weakness or a threat an opportunity. The market perspective allows for both. For example, in the case of your company, its small size could easily be categorized as both a strength and a weakness. The result of the SWOT analysis might look like Figure 5.1

Strengths	Weaknesses
Maintain market share	Jensen becomes direct competitor If released, Jenson's model takes unknown market share
Opportunities	Threats
Small size—flexible, low overhead First to market Strong customer loyalty	Small size—lacking Jensen's resources to reengineer

Figure 5.1 *SWOT Analysis*

If you actually worked in this company, the best advice would be to dust off your résumé because of the threat presented by Jensen. The SWOT analysis makes it clear that your company is simply enjoying the top spot until Jensen, or another as-yet-unknown competitor, steps into the market. Notice as well that the SWOT analysis is a direct example of risk-based thinking. Whenever your company examines threats and weaknesses, consideration of risk is inherent in the process. As your company explores its SWOT factors, it goes without saying that truth and openness are vital to generate the greatest value in the process. The participation of a cross-functional team is as imperative as it is obvious. After all, sales and marketing input is equally important as input related to all elements of SWOT as are manufacturing or "fulfillment" functions. A SWOT analysis created solely by top management will be as unbalanced as one completed exclusively by sales representatives.

Seldom do we find a tool that is a perfect fit, one that fully meets the requirement of a particular clause. SWOT analysis is an excellent tool to satisfy the requirements of clause 4.1.

Clause 4.2: Understanding the Needs and Expectations of Interested Parties

Reason

Understanding the context of your organization is the first step; defining those entities affected by this understanding is the next step, because these groups and individuals represent a significant force of acceptance or argument with regard to your company's strategic direction or products and services. Each interested party has a particular requirement or need that your company is trying to fulfill or recognize in some manner. ISO 9000:2015, the normative reference to ISO 9001:2015, defines both the context of the organization and the interested parties. Paraphrasing item 3.2.3, an *interested party* is a person or organization that can be affected or think of itself as being affected by decisions your company makes or activities it undertakes. Further guidance is available within ISO 9001:2015, Annex A—specifically, Annex A.1, Understanding the Needs and Expectations of Interested Parties. This information is valuable to fully understand how to address this clause specifically because it consistently cautions the user to keep things relevant.

Implementation Guidelines

We suggest that you assemble many of the same people who developed your company's context to develop a list of relevant interested parties (IPs) and what they expect of your products and activities. Many IPs are obvious, three of which are represented in Table 5.1, but your list is certain to be much longer and will likely require considerable thought regarding how to monitor needs or requirements. Regardless, defining your interested parties is the second stage of a larger process whose outcome will feed into clause 4.3, Determining the Scope of the Quality Management System, and clause 4.4, Quality Management System.

Remember that relevance is extremely important, because the list of IPs can be extensive. Take care to not stray too far from the obvious cast of characters, especially those recognized during your development of context. A few examples are provided here:

Table 5.1 *Interested Parties*

Interested Parties	Needs/Requirements	Monitoring Method
Customers	100% quality	Survey Testimonials
Regulatory bodies	100% compliance	Regulator's audits Field performance
Employees	Fair wage Training/personal improvement	Wage surveys Employee reviews
...		

- If the SWOT analysis identified a significant opportunity with two of your current customers, those clients are obviously interested parties.
- If you identified a weakness that one or more market players are exploiting, those companies are interested parties.
- If one of your weaknesses is high turnover, it may require a complete revision of both hiring practices and the training program.
- Your neighborhood is interested in your business as a source of employment but is also concerned with its appearance.
- Regulations are being discussed in Congress that may affect your business, but you do not yet have a working relationship with your local U.S. representative.

Context drives the list of interested parties, essentially moving the thought process from "what" to "who." What do we do or want to do, and who is affected by these drivers?

Clause 4.3: Determining the Scope of the Quality Management System

Reason

Scope sets limits and provides focus. Identifying the scope of any project is the third step in developing your QMS and the first step in its actual implementation. Up to now, you've generated a lot of facts and data. But we've not yet placed parentheses around things, nor have we set boundaries on the day-to-day efforts required to stay in business. You know your context and who's involved, but now you must factor in your products, the processes required to produce them, and whether ISO 9001 requirements impact these processes. Clause 4.3 is also the first mention in the ISO 9001:2015 standard that these decisions must be available as "documented information" (clause 7.3; see Chapter 8) and that the scope includes your QMS's products and services. Furthermore, the scope must include a justification of any ISO 9001 requirement that does not apply to your QMS. (For those who've already developed their QMS, this justification was previously called "exclusions.")

Implementation Guidelines

Since it's required to document scope, we'll use a simple spreadsheet once again to catalogue these forces. Figure 5.2 is a simple representation of Johnson Castings, a metal castings company that has already analyzed its SWOT output and examined the needs of its interested parties. The company noticed that its external issues included a constant problem with poorly written prints, a situation that has plagued it for the last several years. Discussion of this condition led to the realization that it would be much worse if the company had also designed the product it was asked to produce! The quality representative later analyzed ISO 9001:2015 and noticed that clause 8.3, Design, was listed, but obviously the company was glad not to be the designer. The issue of requirements was first mentioned as an external issue and noted as affecting clause 8.3, which was not applicable (N/A). A justification statement followed; it simply noted that Johnson Castings doesn't design any products and that everything it makes is the result of a drawing supplied by its customer. A similar nonapplicable situation arose from the analysis of interested parties, specifically the company's customers, none of which ever asked Johnson Castings to use its own raw materials to produce a casting. This sort of arrangement is referred to as using "property belonging to customers or external providers." In this case, Johnson Castings uses only ingots that it purchases from several trusted suppliers.

There are bound to be many more items populating your spreadsheet, but the most common exclusions are those listed in Figure 5.2: design and the use of customer property. It is not important that a particular nonapplicable clause arise from a specific issue or requirement; rather, the critical point is that your company prepares documented information that represents the analysis of your context and affected interested parties relative to the products you make or services provided.

Johnson Castings		Scope	
Product/Service	Metal Castings	N/A ISO 9001 Clauses	Justification
External issues	▪ Regulations ▪ Customer (porosity) dissatisfaction ▪ Growing market ▪ Influx of unskilled workers ▪ Poorly written customer requirements	8.3: Design and development of products and services	All products are produced using customer-supplied drawings; none is designed by Johnson Castings
Internal issues	▪ Training program ▪ High turnover ▪ Working conditions ▪ Aging equipment	None	
Interested parties' requirements	▪ 100% on-time delivery and quality ▪ Rapid turnaround ▪ Strong community support programs	8.5.3: Property belonging to customers or external providers	All products are produced using ingots purchased by Johnson Castings; customers do not supply raw materials for production use

Figure 5.2 *Scope*

Clause 4.4: The Quality Management System and Its Processes

Reason

We've come full circle from the chapter's beginning as we realize that Deming's words, "If you can't describe what you're doing as a process, you don't know what you're doing," are now driving us to describe not just the processes, but the entire system of processes that constitute your QMS. To "know what you're doing" requires the application of context (clause 4.1), the needs of interested parties (clause 4.2), and scope (clause 4.3) to create an engine that provides consistent, conforming products. The engine is your company, and the important processes within your QMS provide its fuel, monitor its health, and provide information for everyone to make valid decisions.

Implementation

A quality management system is a system of interconnected processes that begin with whatever activities are designed to attract your customers (typically, sales and marketing) and end with the analysis and implementation of improvements needed to further satisfy those customers. Along the way, orders were captured and sent to manufacturing, or in a service organization, incoming calls or direct customer involvement was managed according to predetermined processes. The customer received a "result" or product, be it hardware, software, or information that, if analyzed effectively, was used to revise one or more processes in your operating system to make the next transaction more enjoyable to both the customer and your company. This is why an effective QMS is equivalent to an improvement engine whose fuel is both customer reaction and internal adjustments along the way that improve operational efficiencies.

The ISO 9001:2015 standard requires that your company establish and maintain this system of processes and continually improve its operation. There are eight components to consider, each building atop the next. For ease of implementation, building a flowchart to accomplish the first several components is advised. Figure 5.3 is a very basic rendering of the first two components (your company's chart or process map will undoubtedly be more complex):

- What are the primary processes of your QMS, including their required inputs and expected outputs?
- What is the sequence of these processes, and how are they linked to each other (their interaction)?

Figure 5.3 offers insight into items 1 and 2, the most basic components of a QMS, including inputs and expected outputs for each major process along with defining the linkage and interaction of these processes. Notice that the flowchart also uses ISO 9001 terminology to define these processes. In practice, several subprocesses are likely to be required to comply with other ISO 9001 requirements related to many of these "high-level" process descriptions. Those organizations that use a flowchart or process map will need to expand upon Figure 5.3 or employ a separate spreadsheet to document the next several requirements of clause 4.4:

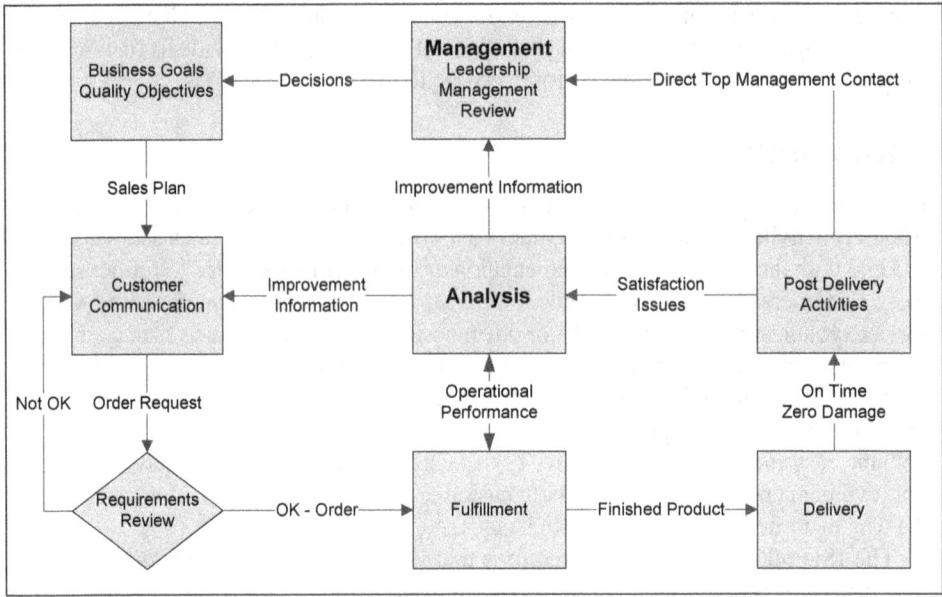

Figure 5.3 *Simple QMS*

- For each major process, which measurements or monitoring controls must be in place to ensure effectiveness? (This may include key performance indicators needed to specify operational effectiveness and control.) How are these metrics monitored?
- Which resources are needed for these processes? Are they available?
- What are the responsibilities and authorities within each process to ensure effective operation?
- Which risks and opportunities apply to one or more processes?

These requirements are principal planning components for a powerful QMS, in that they reduce "good intentions" to metrics and defined responsibilities. Each major process is expected to have one or more metrics that will indicate if it's running as expected. A call center may have as its most critical metric "average wait time," whereas a production facility might use assembly line speed in one operating cell and average final test success metrics in another. Regardless of the metric, the beauty of such a system extends beyond just production activities and into other processes:

- If you (and most organizations should) list purchasing as one of your processes (clause 8.4, Control of Externally Provided Processes, Products, and Services), metrics for effectiveness could include goals for supplier performance, annual purchasing expenditure reduction goals, and reduction of the overall supply base by a defined percentage.

- Shipping may have its metric of 100 percent accuracy in shipping documentation augmented by reducing the cost of packaging materials by a defined percentage while also reducing damaged goods.
- Design, within its many steps, might use defined metrics to note its ability to meet target dates for key phases of a new design.

Do not use systemic metrics to represent the performance of a particular process! Systemic metrics such as 100 percent on-time delivery or 100 percent quality are the result of many processes working together to achieve these results. No single process can represent the efforts of many, so be certain to examine each process as a contributor, making its own unique donation to these overall or systemic goals.

Finally, a method must be developed to make certain these metrics are reviewed on a regular basis. Given that such metrics provide a clear indication of the performance of each process and how well the processes are collectively progressing toward an overall result, this information is timely and should not be consigned to a semi-annual report. Monitoring should instead be based on importance of the data and other concerns, especially those having a direct effect on customers.

Of course, nothing works without resources, be they time, materials, or people—and processes are no different. Depending on the process and what it must accomplish (its "result" or output), any number of resources may be necessary to maintain or improve the process's performance. Because of the importance of resources, these items are linked in that someone or some department is responsible for managing them and making sure they remain available to those who need them. For example, a production floor needs tools and machinery as its primary resources. Tools required for manufacturing are listed in a separate machinery log. While the production manager is responsible for ensuring that those tools are properly used and maintained, the ultimate authority for machine condition is the maintenance department. As a second example, consider that the design department's primary resource might be the computer system and several important pieces of software. These items were purchased under the authority of the design manager, and the information technology (IT) department manages their seamless integration within the overall IT system.

A new clause in ISO 9001 introduces the concept of risk and opportunities, or "risk-based thinking." While this subject is described in greater detail in Chapter 7's examination of clause 6.1, Actions to Address Risks and Opportunities, we need to preface this discussion with a brief introduction of both risk and "objectives," another requirement explained in clause 6.2.

Your company is expected to answer the question, "Which risks and opportunities apply to one or more processes?" Thus far, we've been building a spreadsheet to define each element of clause 4.4, and the next two columns are directly related to the *risks and opportunities* within each process to *achieve your objectives*. We previously noted that a QMS requires your company to provide resources to enable these processes to achieve several goals and to monitor performance. These departmental or process-level goals are based on analysis of context and interested parties, just as high-level goals ("objectives") are developed to centralize activities of all these processes to achieve the same systemic outcome.

Objectives

Perhaps it becomes clear as a result of all the analysis that your company has decided that that speed, or "time to market," is central to remain competitive, as is price. Objectives 1 and 2 would therefore become "speed" and "cost." Suppose that further analysis indicates that intense training, safety, and employee retention are required throughout the company to achieve these objectives. A third objective might then be called "people." These three objectives then become central to all activities in the company, and metrics are established to monitor progress toward individual goals within each process that contribute to one or all of these objectives. Objectives are necessary to succeed and when regularly monitored, provide valuable information to everyone, especially top management as it seeks to determine whether additional resources are needed to support the goals of each contributing process. These objectives are often posted on performance boards within the facility with metrics, or key performance indicators (KPIs), appropriately assigned to each. There is great opportunity in each objective to centralize activities and maintain focus. Developing and achieving the right objectives is key to achieving success in regard to the overall business plan.

Risk

Unfortunately, the opposite is also true: Not achieving your objectives can lead to underperformance and any number of negative consequences. At the highest level, "risk" can be defined as not achieving your objectives. Developing objectives is an example of "risk-based thinking" as management looks across its context and interested parties to decide what's important to sustainability or growth and success in a particular business. Objectives set the course of a company's journey as means to contain or avoid anticipated risk. Their risk-based importance is why the metrics of each department are monitored closely on a regular basis.

Your spreadsheet of elements within your QMS now adds one additional column: risk and opportunities (R&O) related to your objectives. Here's how this works: For each process, analyze its strongest link to one or more objectives and note which is most appropriate to each process. For instance, referring back to the earlier example of speed, cost, and people objectives, the purchasing group is focused primarily on cost. Cost containment and reduction is its greatest contribution; it offers an important opportunity to maintain margins but represents a high risk if the cost of raw materials continues to rise. Cost is entered in the purchasing process's row.

Similarly, the shipping department is primarily focused on speed, accuracy, and safety. This process is noted as closely related to both people and speed. (Yes, a process may be managing the dual edge of risk and opportunity for one or even all objectives in your company!) The human resources department addresses the people objective, and so on. As each of these processes is added into it, the QMS spreadsheet becomes a powerful tool to see "at a glance" how each process is designed to work with other processes and how all processes are intended to accomplish the same objectives. As you review Figure 5.4, remember that your spreadsheet will likely be far more detailed and precise.

Process Sequence	KPIs	Monitoring Method	Resources	Responsibility	Risks and Opportunities*
Management	On-time decisions Quarterly all-employee reports	Semi-annual review	Office related	President	S, C, G, P
Human resources	>10% turnover HR software implementation Q4	Monthly review	Office related 6 staff	HR director	P
Sales	10% annual sales growth >3% order errors	Monthly review	Office related Sales fleet 12 staff	Sales director	G
Engineering	98% on-time drawings	Monthly review	Office related 9 staff	Engineering director	S, C
Purchasing	12% cost of goods sold reduction	Monthly review	Office related 7 staff	Purchasing director	C
Production Planning	>8 hours to schedule production	Monthly review	Office related 4 staff	Planning manager	S, C
Production	100% quality 100% on-time	Monthly review	Office related See machine listing 43 staff	Production manager	C, G, P
Warehouse	5S program implementation by Q4	Monthly review	Office related Forklifts 7 staff	Warehouse manager	C
Shipping	>2% error rate	Monthly review	Office related Forklifts 7 staff	Shipping manager	C

*Applied to objectives of speed (S), cost (C), growth (G), and people (P).

Figure 5.4 *QMS*

DetailProcess performance monitoring and improvement is also accomplished through other requirements within ISO 9001:2015, including the following:

- Internal audit (clause 9.2)
- Management review (clause 9.3)
- Control of nonconforming outputs (clause 8.7)
- Analysis and evaluation (clause 9.1.3)
- Nonconformity and corrective action (clause 10.2)

Two other clauses in ISO 9001:2015 are often referred to as the "act" segment of the PDCA cycle, wherein a company has already set a plan in motion and is ready to analyze its success, including possible alterations to its original plan:

- Analyze the success of these processes to then make necessary changes so that these processes perform as expected, or "achieve intended results" (clause 4.4.1g)
- Enact process improvements and thereby improve the quality management system. (clause 4.4.1f)

Now the QMS is ready. These two additional clauses (the "act" segment) are implemented through a number of interconnected processes called out in the ISO 9001 standard. For example, internal audit (clause 9.2) and management review (clause 9.3) are tools that collect process performance information; if their outcomes fall shy of the expected results, they call attention to the problem so that the organization can start correcting or improving the situation. Control of nonconforming outputs (clause 8.7), analysis and evaluation (clause 9.1.3), and nonconformity and corrective action (clause 10.2) are directly related to improving operations and process performance.

So far, we've set the stage for further definition of your QMS and even jumped ahead a bit to incorporate objectives and risk-based thinking to develop your quality system. The next major clause of ISO 9001:2015 was once called "Management Responsibility" and was for many years thought to be a reasonable expression of those things managers should set in place to ensure a successful QMS. As the next chapter will show, that understanding is no longer considered enough; the new clause 5 will surely require a great deal of negotiation and patience for those individuals whose top managers were not fully engaged in the operation and success of their QMS.

6

Clause 5: Leadership

ISO 9001:2015 reaches higher than previous editions of the standard in relation to management responsibilities. In the past, managers were primarily required to provide resources for the quality management system. The unintended result of this approach was to separate business concerns from quality concerns, though clearly the two have and will always be linked. For those new to the ISO 9001 standard, this change has no relevance, as you will be embarking on a process of developing a system for leaders whose attention is equally devoted to business and quality. In contrast, for those who have developed a separate quality function that primarily interacts with top management through annual management reviews, additional requirements have been added that must be addressed. The new leader is not simply committed, but rather intimately involved—something that implies action and deeds not previously addressed in earlier editions of the standard. Likewise, just as the top manager is now more than ever involved in quality, so the quality manager or director is now more involved in business.

Clause 5.1: Leadership and Commitment

Reason

The members of the working group that developed the requirements for leadership were mindful of past omissions and their consequences. Previous revisions of ISO 9001 were far less prescriptive in regard to management's role in support of a quality management system (QMS). The 2015 revision clarifies not only those areas that management must support, but also requires that there be no distinction between "business" and "quality" requirements.

Previous revisions of ISO 9001 made it possible for companies to effectively manage two systems: one directed toward operational quality and improvement, typically managed by the quality department, and the business plan designed to achieve overall financial success through careful attention to sales goals. Of course, the functional separation of sales and quality is a traditional one, with each having its own unique perspective. Though cartoonish, imagine a "mom and pop" corner store in which the extroverted, proud, and knowledgeable shop owner is in near-constant conflict and disagreement with his introverted and concerned wife, whose job is to tend to the disciplines of bookkeeping, inventory, logistics, and little else. The concerns expressed by the dutiful wife can be ignored for a while, but her extroverted husband eventually has to admit to her that taxes, insurance issues, and many other good business requirements are just as important as a smile and handshake for customers entering their shop. It may be true that "The quality department's concerns are important, but without sales, there wouldn't be a quality department!," but it is equally true that given enough time, this argument eventually breaks down. Without good quality, sales will dry up, customers will leave, and businesses will go under. The business and quality realms are inseparable and supportive of each other.

The current model of a separate, central administration composed of a company's president, chief executive officer (CEO), chief financial officer (CFO), and various vice presidents is all too typical in large companies. Of course, smaller operations may not have sufficient resources to afford a separate building for their top management, but these top managers most often work in a segregated area in close proximity to each other. Regardless of whether it is intended, the net effect is to project these leaders' status and importance, which in turn insulates operations from them. This separation inherently creates a range of tensions that inhibit open and effective communication within the company, especially when each group uses different terminology to describe their primary concerns or methods.

With the release of ISO 9001:2015, organizations are no longer able to designate quality as a discipline managed by a particular department, occasionally reporting on its successes or challenges to top management. The new approach of "marrying business and quality" is now clearly articulated (see especially clause 5.1d), requiring "integration of the quality management system requirements into the organization's business processes."

Implementation

Implementation of clause 5.1 might best be addressed in a sequential manner. There are 10 requirements (5.1a–j) relative to which top management is required to "demonstrate leadership and commitment." Take each requirement as it comes through a succession of meetings to explain each concept and draft actionable activities. Involvement will be key to success, as the first hurdle will be to define "top" management in the first place. ISO 9000:2015 defines a *top manager* as a "person or group of people who directs and controls an organization at the highest level." While this may not be the most desirable definition because it tells us little that we don't already know, a key concept to consider is "direction and control at the highest level." Denizens of the "C-Suite" (i.e., those with titles such as CEO or president) are obvious candidates. Those at the highest level report to the fewest masters, but have power and influence over the largest number of employees and other interested parties.

Clause 5.1a: Accountable for Effectiveness

The first requirement, clause 5.1a, requires top managers to demonstrate their leadership and commitment to being accountable for the effectiveness of the quality management system. If someone is accountable, he or she is held responsible—in this case, accountable to the effectiveness of the QMS. In most companies, accountability for the effectiveness of the QMS has not been the responsibility of top management, but rather assigned to the quality director or quality manager. Of course, top management is ultimately responsible for virtually everything in the company, delegating specialty responsibilities to lower-level, trusted managers. The 2015 standard does not require that the company's leader become both president and quality director, but rather maintains that she is now responsible for the effectiveness of the QMS. Some will rightly argue that this individual was always accountable for the effectiveness of the QMS, just as she is accountable for the success or failure of every department. However, the QMS is a special responsibility, one calling for active involvement to the extent that its success or failure is attributable to at least the designated quality manager/director *and* the chief executive.

All 10 requirements within clause 5.1 require that top managers demonstrate leadership and commitment—in this case, to the effectiveness of the QMS. But how are these requirements demonstrated? The following are possible tangible activities:

- Conduct regular, open meetings with all employees regarding the importance, current status, and challenges of the OMS. Retain PowerPoint slides or written agendas as documented information.
- Add accountability for the effectiveness of the QMS to the job descriptions of one or more chief executives.
- Add one or more chief executives to the roster of several standing meetings where quality is the primary subject:
  - Nonconformance and corrective action review meetings
  - Quality department planning meetings
  - Employee-level ("tool box") meetings regarding quality problems/issues
- Conduct performance reviews of top management's direct reports based primarily on their department's ability to meet business/quality objectives.
- Rename the "quality manual" as the "business manual."

Clause 5.1b: Develop and Maintain the Quality Policy and Objectives to Be Compatible with Context (4.1) and Strategic Direction

Clause 5.1c: Ensuring the Integration of QMS Requirements into Your Business Processes

Clause 5.1b is the first of several requirements intended to unite business and quality into a single system. This is destined be a delicate balancing act in those companies that have built silo walls around the quality department or the activities of top management, because clauses 5.1b and 5.1c are designed to minimize functional isolation between the activities of each group. Now that you've defined context (clause 4.1), the standard asks that these insights become the foundation for strategic direction, or long-term goal setting. Strategic planning has traditionally been the responsibility of top management, though many companies enlist the ideas of all departments in developing the plan. Armed with the strategic plan, the company then develops or strengthens (provides additional resources for) several business processes. These "business processes" are no different from any process previously discussed in Chapter 4, but simply carry the qualifier of "business." (A process, regardless of its name, transforms one or more inputs into one or more outputs.) At a minimum, if your organization adopts the idea of renaming your quality manual as a business manual, all process can then be considered to be business processes. Developing the quality/business policy and resulting objectives to support the strategic plan finalizes proof of top management's commitment to compliance with clauses 5.1b and 5.1c.

These two clauses are examples of ISO's overarching effort to standardize the language and structure of management systems standards through the use of what's called the "high-level structure" in Annex SL of the ISO directives. These clauses are course corrections because, as mentioned earlier, the traditional separation between quality and top management has been maintained in the majority of companies ever since ISO 9001 was launched in 1987. In 2015, clauses 5.1b and 5.1c should put an end to the often-heard lament that quality improvement is never successful when top management is unsupportive or ambivalent; business management and quality management simply can't be separate functions anymore.

Clause 5.1d: The Process Approach and Risk-Based Thinking

The Process Approach

The requirement for top management to demonstrate leadership and commitment to clauses 5.1d and 5.1e may require some degree of training. The concepts of process approach and risk-based thinking are presented in ISO 9000:2015 and are necessary for you to understand before engaging top management in the change effort. Neither is exceptionally difficult to comprehend: The process approach recognizes that all processes consist of inputs that are transformed into outputs, with both inputs and outputs being measurable, and that processes are most always connected, such that the output of one process becomes the input to the next. The output of each process is its "planned result," and results measurements most closely aligned with your company's objectives are of primary importance. In fact, these results provide an early warning system when regularly monitored, as a slowdown of one process causes the next process in line (and all subsequent processes) to also slow its pace. As depicted in Figure 6.1, a process also requires resources to operate and controls to protect these resources and the activities of transforming an input into an output such as inspections and tests. All process activities function in balance with one another when the company's operations are most effective. Management expresses commitment to the process approach by embracing the concepts of requiring process definition as well as effective process monitoring.

Figure 6.1 is simply a basic depiction of a process, the foundation of the process approach; the reader is encouraged to search the web for more detailed information. The interaction of processes in your company is vital to your success in meeting your objectives. As mentioned earlier, management expresses commitment to the process approach by embracing the concepts of requiring process definition as well as effective process monitoring. Those companies that regularly analyze "process KPIs," throughput metrics, and similar criteria connected to process performance are already on the right track.

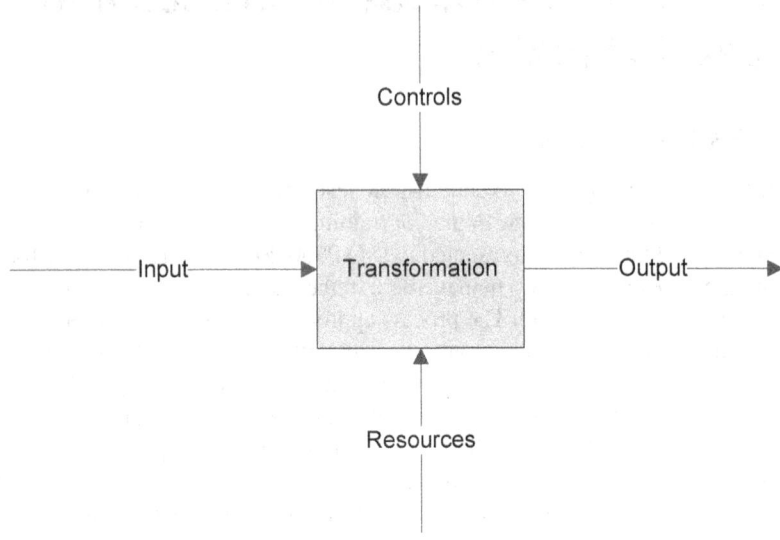

Figure 6.1 *Process Approach*

Risk-Based Thinking

Risk-based thinking is new to the ISO 9001 standard and has its origins in "preventive action," which is no longer a formal requirement. By most accounts, the failure of preventive action was rooted in its inability to find universal implementation throughout ISO 9001's user base. Instead, it became a lesser component of corrective action, languishing in a permanent rear position within the QMS.

When you step back and analyze your typical workday, most of your daily activities can be traced to the effort to prevent a negative outcome. Scheduling meetings are not held to ensure that packages arrive late to the customer, and neither are most planning events throughout the business day that seek to enable flow and positive results. When seen from this perspective, these events are actions to prevent a negative outcome, or simply preventive actions, based on your company's understanding of potential risk(s). These actions therefore represent "risk-based thinking." Certainly, conducting a formal failure-mode effects analysis (FMEA) is pure risk analysis. The reason for undertaking FMEA is to examine specific actions or activities that might be difficult to accomplish and then plug in one or more preventive activities to avoid possible problems before starting a project. This, however, is not risk-based thinking as intended by the ISO 9001:2015 standard. Instead, FMEA can be viewed as a formal process of risk analysis and avoidance. FEMA is not required to be compliant with the concept of thinking from the perspective of risk. Instead, it takes only a minute to ask if all the appropriate risks have been addressed before starting a particular project, especially in relation to context and interested parties. Annex A of ISO 9001:2015 makes it clear that there is "no requirement for formal methods for risk management or a documented risk management process," strengthening the concept that management need simply demonstrate leadership and commitment by encouraging everyone in the company to adopt a new standard of risk-based thinking. Compliance is achieved when risk becomes embedded in the thinking of the organization through organization and regular reporting of the status of important processes to top management.

Clause 5.1e: Availability of Resources for the QMS

Effective resource management, introduced in clause 5.1e, calls for top management to provide the necessary time, materials, people, and funding for the QMS to succeed. Now that the QMS is synonymous with the business system, resources needed throughout the company must be both available and appropriate to maintain expected results of the QMS and for the company as a whole to succeed and prosper according to a strategic plan. Numerous forces may change the profiles of the various departments throughout the year. Additional business, the acquisition of new machinery or software, and the departure of several veteran employees, for example, can stretch the abilities of any expected result (process output). Compliance with this subclause can be demonstrated through constant corrections based on process monitoring that ensure the appropriate resources are in place, which in turn demonstrates leadership and commitment to maintaining process excellence.

Clauses 5.1f–j

The remaining subclauses in clause 5 are invitations to meet with managers and discuss methods to demonstrate leadership and commitment to a variety of specific responsibilities that, in the end, involve nothing more than being best stewards to those whose work affects product or service quality. The goal of all 5.1 subclauses is to move top management's attention and activities from those of an observer to those of a participant. A participant demonstrates leadership and commitment through actions, not just words. To be most effective, restructuring an existing QMS to comply with ISO 9001:2015 would be best served by starting with the whole of clause 5, because the implementation of all "new requirements" in the standard ultimately requires the leadership and commitment of top management. Clause 4 defines your company; clause 5 defines how best to focus and engage everyone in the company, starting at the top.

Clause 5.2: Quality Policy
Reason

Once again, top management is required to demonstrate leadership and commitment to the concept of "customer focus." ISO 9001 has used this term in the past in relation to top management; it differs from "customer satisfaction" in that "focus" should be the groundwork for "satisfaction." Top management's role in satisfying the customer is therefore to encourage the company to focus on the customer's wants and needs, because they are the fundamental underpinnings of satisfaction. This is not a new requirement, but one that has been routinely misunderstood. The reason for an organization to be customer focused is not simply to state the obvious, but rather to formally ensure that processes are designed according to fundamental customer needs and wants that include legal issues, risk, and attentiveness to customers' perception of your products and services.

Implementation: Statutory and Regulatory Requirements

The three subclauses within clause 5.2 relate to statutory and regulatory requirements, risk, and the company's ability to enhance customer satisfaction whenever possible. Statutory and regulatory requirements are essentially the legal requirements to maintain your business. In the case of a very small business, the number of legal issues is typically small. Other than abiding by customs requirements when shipping their products out of the country, and adhering to occupational safety and health and possibly environmental regulations, small businesses rarely face the onslaught of regulations typically encountered by multinational organizations and large businesses. For the latter enterprises, it may be necessary to retain attorneys or invest in whole departments whose sole responsibility is to ensure that statutory and regulatory requirements are considered and managed most effectively. Demonstrating leadership regarding statutory and regulatory requirements starts with top management's clear and decisive call to never disregard the legal requirements within the client relationship. There are no "workarounds" to lawful business practices, and to be most effective the sales and marketing departments must play an integral role in identifying and communicating legal concerns between the customer and the organization.

Risks and Opportunities

The second element of customer focus, as defined in clause 5.2b, is top management's leadership in communicating the importance of determining both the risks and the opportunities that the organization's products or services contribute to what you've determined is important in satisfying the customer. While the writers of the 2015 edition of

ISO 9001 chose to identify risk as the opposite of opportunity, many within the risk management world argue that they are two sides of the same coin. Their position is that risk is a component of any opportunity, and that some risks are positive, as in the often-stated maxim of investing, "The greater the risk, the greater the opportunity!" Regardless your position, risk and opportunity imply both a negative outcome and a positive outcome are possible results of whatever the product or experience offers the customer (Table 6.1). Customers buy your goods or services because they chose to or have experienced your QMS's ability to achieve consistent, conforming products. Leaders must demonstrate leadership and commitment to defining the basis of that choice, or what your customer wants, and maximizing these criteria to improve the customer experience.

Table 6.1 *Risk and Opportunity*

Risk	Opportunity
Automobile crashes	Automobile transports in luxury
Doughnut adds fat cells	Doughnut tastes wonderful
Caffeine affects heart rate	Coffee tastes wonderful
Exercise is boring	Exercise promotes health
Boating is expensive	Boating is relaxing and fun
The software gathers personal information	The software makes it easy to buy products

The simplest way to describe how to maintain customer focus is through your company's "value proposition." The risk of losing focus on your value proposition—that is, on what your organization does best and for what it is primarily noticed in the market—can be disastrous. These qualities define your products and services; your value proposition, in turn, solidifies your company's place in the market. "Value proposition" is a term that top management readily identifies with and encompasses all considerations of both risk and opportunity. The value proposition is the totality of what your organization does and the customer's experience with your products. It can be improved, but its basic functionality of providing a readily identifiable opportunity to the customer will always be deeply rooted in your company's processes and results.

As an example, a ladder is an essential tool to enable a worker to reach items at heights beyond the individual's normal reach—certainly a great opportunity in and of itself. But it's also true that workers routinely fall off ladders and that any ladder manufacturing company must do all it can to alert users of this risk and design a safer product. The customer wants the ability to work safely (opportunity) at heights above normal reach (risk). The company that creates the safest and easiest-to-use ladder has defined a powerful value proposition; its customer focus recognizes the risks and opportunities, and management is responsible for demonstrating leadership and commitment to the process. By extension, all products and services share the same concept of risk and opportunity. (Universal to advertising is the reality that opportunities are always identified and promoted as counteracting or outweighing risks!)

Customer Satisfaction

The final element of customer focus, clause 5.2c, is a call for top management's leadership in communicating the importance of maintaining customer satisfaction. The functional equivalent of maintaining satisfaction is not to deviate from what works. Standards are written to promote trade, but there will be no trade if your products or services are substandard. Those organizations that provide consistent results will become known for their reliability; when this reliability is matched with conformance to what the customer wants, the result is satisfied customers. Demands on process outputs to reduce costs that in turn compromise the company's ability to provide consistent results, or design changes that challenge the consumer to adapt to a new product or service but yield little or no gain erode continued satisfaction—yet they still happen every day. The role of top management is to be watchful and provide stewardship in maintaining the company's value proposition.

Clause 5.2.1: Policy

Reason

Top management is responsible for setting policies that affect the entire company in regard to working hours, vacations, benefits, and any number of similar rules for all employees to follow. The same principle holds for the development of the quality policy, in that it applies to everyone and everything in the company. A strong and meaningful quality policy has the ability to establish a tone and direction within the company that encourages excellence, creates momentum, reaches people intellectually, and creates a common purpose.

Implementation

The quality policy is supposed to be appropriate to the context and strategic direction as well as the overriding purpose of your company. At this point, we've discussed context and strategic direction, aided by use of the SWOT analysis as suggested in Chapter 5. The concept of purpose is embedded in this work, and is perhaps obvious by now. However, a company's purpose is often elusive simply because it is so obvious:

- A major soft drink manufacturer was tentative about adding bottled water to its product mix until it realized that the company's essential purpose was to quench thirst.
- A medical device company is famous for its logo that depicts a patient rising from his hospital bed.
- The CEO of a steel fabrication plant in the Midwest always prefaces any public remarks by stating that his company "shelters businesses."

When developing the quality policy, a solid understanding of purpose, context, and strategic direction is essential to all subsequent considerations. Without these bedrock, foundational underpinnings, the policy will sound hollow and to many, will be just "words on paper." Developing the policy is as important as developing values, mission, and vision statements. If your company decides to develop one or more of these statements, we advise that the quality policy be last in the sequence. The quality policy is in many respects the most direct of these types of statements and is best perceived as a call for action once vision and mission are finalized.

The policy must also "provide a framework" for developing your company's quality objectives. Think of the policy as the skeleton while objectives are the flesh and blood of a QMS. If the policy emphasizes speed and efficiency, the objectives should include metrics to monitor velocity and/or improvements in output. Thus, while a policy states what is important, objectives indicate how to achieve it. If the policy makes it clear why the company is dedicated to a certain level of excellence, objectives should be written to achieve standards of quality and perhaps appearance.

The quality policy must also include the company's commitment to satisfying requirements and improving the QMS. (Both are actually embedded in the ISO 9001:2015 standard, as clauses 8 and 10 deal with defining requirements and improvement, respectively.) The quality policy must be complete, clear, and concise; easy to understand; and often repeated. Further information will follow in the next subclause, "Communicating the Quality Policy," but to aid in developing your quality policy, we offer the following guidance:

- The policy should be written in clearly understandable language. Test draft policies by asking representatives throughout the company for comment. If something is not easily understood, it should be revised.
- A quality policy introduces a new language, one of quality management and improvement. Choose your words wisely, because changing language changes culture. If, for example, the term "associates" is used to describe fellow employees in your policy, no doubt employees will soon start using that term. In this instance, ask yourself if "associates" is preferable to "partners" or some other expression. The most meaningful quality policy is destined to be referred to by many throughout the workday. Be aware during its development that the words you use must be repeatable by everyone.

- A quality policy is typically posted throughout the company and on its website. As completion nears, be sure to include considerations of typeface and format. A powerfully presented quality Policy is that much closer to communicating its importance.

Top management is responsible for developing the quality policy, in part as the summation of the organization's reason to exist and a beacon for sustainability. The particulars are important because it's a lasting call to excellence. Objectives will be accomplished and replaced by new ones, but the policy lives on.

Clause 5.2.2: Communicating the Quality Policy

Reason

The quality policy is a tool. Of course, any tool is meaningless unless it is applied and used as intended. Companies that truly commit to their quality policy constantly find new and creative ways to weave its content and meaning into their everyday operations. In good times and bad, the quality policy should provide direction for decision making and serve as a constant reminder of the organization's path to improvement.

Implementation

Certainly, the policy must be available for people to reference. Posting it throughout the company is common practice, and we strongly suggest that you do so in your lobby as well. Posting this policy in the lobby can set a foundational tone and principles of interaction between your company and those from outside. Many comment that the quality policy is often the first topic of conversation if it's available for vendors and customers to read while waiting for their meeting or contact person.

Top management may have created the policy, but these leaders should not rely on others to communicate its importance, even though the standard does not make such a distinction. Top managers have an obligation to ensure that the quality policy is understood as they understand it. In other words, the message is delivered in two parts—content and intent—and both are equally important.

Another consideration within this clause is that top managers need to address how to apply the quality policy. The brief explanation of how to apply the quality policy is "everywhere!" It opens every meeting as the first PowerPoint slide; it hangs as a banner from the ceiling of the production floor; and it is formally framed and prominently placed in every conference room. There is no end to its "application," in that this policy is the fastest and most direct way to communicate what an organization stands for and promises to accomplish, regardless of title, department, or job description. In addition, when the quality policy is openly displayed, it becomes available to anyone interested in learning about it. This is the final requirement of communicating the policy and if it's displayed virtually everywhere in some form or another, compliance is easily demonstrated.

Clause 5.3: Organizational Roles, Responsibilities, and Authorities

Reason

A final requirement of top management is that everyone in an organization understand his or her contribution to the QMS through the individual's everyday work and reporting. Each of us has a unique role to play, much as any sports team assigns positions and trains its players accordingly to win the game. The contribution of each player is understood according to his position on the team, and everyone is made aware of the rules of the game and the requirements of playing within those rules. It's no different for any organization: Each contributor must be aware of the requirements of the QMS and her respective role and responsibilities within it. And just as a sports team's coach is ultimately responsible for positioning and monitoring each player, so the ISO 9001:2015 standard requires that top management make sure that work assignments are clearly communicated and understood throughout the company.

Clauses 5.3a–e

The ISO 9001:2015 standard lists five components of defining roles, responsibilities, and authorities in determining who is responsible and/or authorized to handle the following activities:

- Make certain that the company is compliant with ISO 9001:2015
- Monitor processes to ensure that they are operating as planned
- Report to top management regarding overall QMS performance
- Maintain customer focus
- In the event of change, make sure that the QMS is not disrupted or harmed

The traditional approach is to assign all of these duties to members of the quality department. Previous editions of the standard listed these assignments under the heading of the "Management Representative." This title is no longer mentioned, having been dropped in the 2015 edition in part to encourage more of a team approach to managing the QMS—that is, an approach that is inclusive of more than one person or department. Of course, assigning one person or department to continue managing these five requirements is unquestionably compliant with the standard, but the reader is encouraged to think deeply about other possibilities. Perhaps the quality manager is responsible, but the president holds authority for one or all requirements, thereby demonstrating top management commitment. Alternatively, perhaps the president or other top management position holds responsibility and authority to maintain customer focus, while another position is tasked with monitoring processes to ensure that they are operating as planned.

We are confident that the inclusive approach, especially in light of the need for top management to demonstrate its commitment to the QMS, is a decided improvement from earlier editions of the standard. A simple QMS organizational chart or spreadsheet would suffice to record these assignments as documented information, though it's not a listed requirement to do so. However, such a tool would certainly come in handy in the event of an audit, and it represents an excellent way to get the initial discussion started among all the intended players. Dispersing these important duties, and thereby creating a team approach with the inclusion of top management, creates the strength and clarity needed for the work ahead.

7

Clause 6: Planning for the Quality Management System

Regardless of the reason, cutting corners in planning of any business-related activity is surely a formula that will generate the ultimate result of total disaster. Clause 6 of ISO 9001:2015 addresses planning of your quality management system (QMS) and changes to it, along with considering associated risks and opportunities to obtain the desired consequences and continual improvement.

Determining the architecture of any management system requires identifying the activities that must be performed to ensure all key processes are understood by employees, employees are trained to follow the processes, and processes are adhered to achieve planned results. The planned results for QMSs vary widely from one company to another. Likewise, the scope of these systems differs based on the organization's size, its customers, the country where the organization resides, and the industry sector pursued by the company (e.g., telecommunications, financial, health care). In addition, variations to QMSs can be company-wide or occur within individual functions on an organization-wide basis. The outcome that companies most commonly seek is to ensure that quality objectives are met and their products or services consistently meet customer and necessary regulatory requirements.

Clause 6.1: Actions to Address Risks and Opportunities

The initiation phase of a QMS lays the core foundation for this system and requires consideration of all aspects of planning, based on the strategic direction of the organization as far as the product or service is concerned. During this phase, it is essential to ensure QMS risks are identified up-front to avoid any undesirable effects. The most common reasons for the failure of a QMS include the following:

- Failure to understand who the customer is
- Failure to understand the needs of customers as they relate to industry and regulatory requirements
- Failure to determine impacts
- Lack of and/or failure to adhere to process
- Lack of communication at all levels of the organization
- Absence of clear roles and associated responsibilities

ISO 9001:2015 places a greater emphasis on understanding the customer and the customer's needs vis-à-vis industry and regulatory requirements. Both of these factors need to be considered very early on in the creation and planning of the QMS. The revised standard does not specify that a formal risk management plan must be implemented. However, once the risks are identified, it does require actions to address those risks. Here it is important to point out that risks can also lead to opportunities. For example, if your company manufactures a medical product (device) that monitors blood pressure, the associated risk is the device not reading the blood pressure correctly, which in certain circumstances can lead to a stroke if the blood pressure is very high. However, the opportunities are also numerous: For example, the blood pressure monitor might indicate he high blood pressure faster than competing models, thereby providing information needed for the patient to obtain the necessary treatment.

Another example of risk and opportunities arises in the telecommunications industry, where large organizations often have several partners that sell their products. The risk is that if the partners are not trained adequately regarding sales and support of the product, the partnership will experience diminishing returns. Conversely, there is a tremendous opportunity for the partners to do their own advertising, sell several units of the product, provide customer training, offer post-sale support, and gain a larger market share for the product.

Reason

For many companies, staying abreast of global and domestic competition and meeting customer demands that are growing more intense each year have become challenging in recent years. Industry and regulatory requirements have also increased, which places added pressure on participants in many industries. These combined forces are driving organizations to place extra emphasis on, and devote more time and money to, their QMS in a quest to improve their operating efficiencies. Every organization that offers products or services does so with the intention of garnering growth in sales, and such growth is evidenced by wide acceptance of their products or services by consumers.

For an organization to grow, it must take risks. For example, there may be a need to acquire another business to grow the purchasing organization. When such a need arises, comprehensive analysis of the risks and opportunities must be conducted to avoid traumatic effects, especially in the areas of merging the two organizational cultures, training sales personnel, and dealing with the departure of customers and talented personnel from the acquired company. Among other collateral benefits, successful implementation of the QMS may result in a gain in market share, an increased customer base, positive brand recognition, and realization of a competitive advantage.

Implementation Guidelines

The generic meaning of "planning" for the QMS is the process of identifying your quality objectives, developing plans to meet those objectives, and implementing the plans to obtain the goals you are looking for. Figure 7.1 highlights common high-level steps completed for the QMS. Each of these steps will require additional related activities. In Figure 7.1, only "product" is mentioned, but the same steps can be used for "service" as well.

First, you must develop a flowchart of the processes, identifying the dependencies and the sequence of the processes. Next, identify the inputs and outputs for each process. Identify the risks that might prevent you from obtaining the desired results from the QMS, and then develop strategies to address these risks. Finally, evaluate the opportunities that may prove beneficial to the organization. We will discuss the goals later in this chapter, in the context of clause 6.2.

Within an organization, the quality plans are interconnected. Thus it is necessary to have broad quality objectives at the top of the organization and then break these objectives into individual activities and subactivities as they filter through individual functional areas. Once the activities of the QMS are identified, along with the other requirements stated in clause 4.4, you need to start planning the order in which activities will take place, their interrelationships, and their interactions. In addition, you must specify who will do the activities, how the results will be evaluated, and how success will be measured.

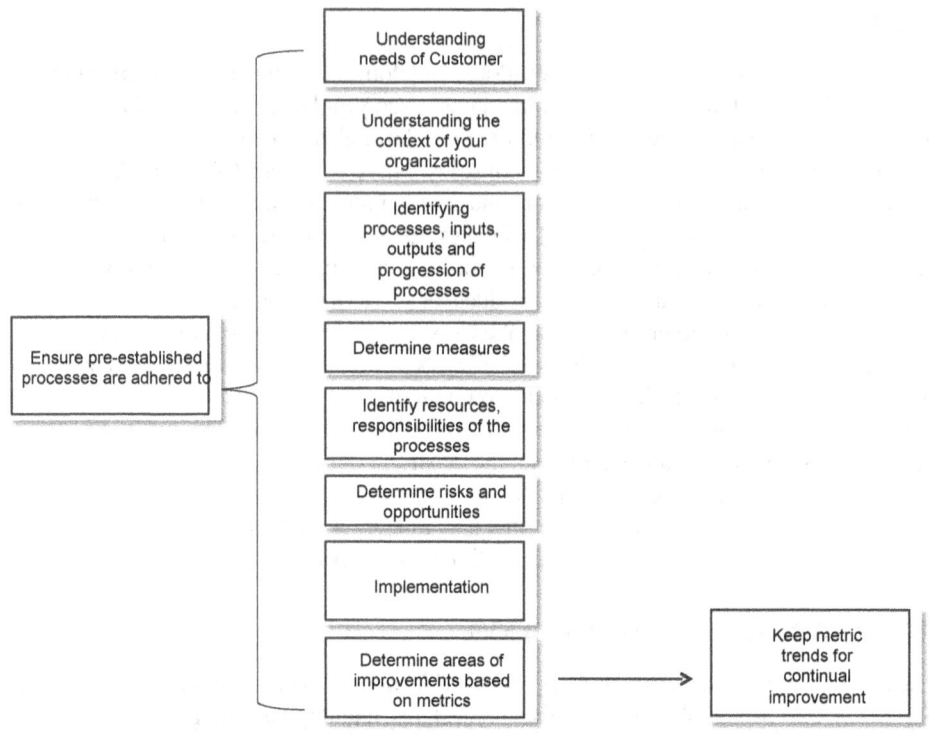

Figure 7.1 *High-Level QMS Planning Roadmap*

Clause 6.2: Quality Objectives and Planning to Achieve Them

Every stakeholder in your company must be involved in the development of the QMS and its implementation plans, and each must be consulted as the system evolves. It is crucial to create an in-depth communication plan for this purpose. Moreover, it should be made clear throughout the organization that customer satisfaction, not simply financial gain, is the ultimate goal. Your organization's strategic quality plans and business plans must be inseparable—the QMS plans must be incorporated into your business strategy and objectives.

There is often confusion about the difference between the objectives and the goals within quality systems. As an example, if the objective is to identify customers, then the goal might be to develop a list of the customers. Another objective might be to develop a product; in that case, the goal might be to identify and develop product features. The requirement of clause 6.2 is that the organization establish quality objectives that are harmonious or coherent with its quality policy.

The quality objectives must be consistently examined, communicated, and revised as necessary to achieve the intended results of obtaining best-in-class customer satisfaction. The objectives have to be related to the product and also in accord with the products and services if the organization is to continuously increase customer satisfaction. From a legal standpoint, verbal objectives are just as valid as written ones, but the problem is overcoming the burden of proof when no documentation exists. For this reason, ISO 9001:2015 requires you to retain documented information on quality objectives.

Clause 6.2 states clearly that the quality objectives for appropriate functions have to be in sync with the organization's quality policy, be measurable, and be pertinent to the organization's products and services and to customer satisfaction.

In today's constantly changing business environment, it is vital to monitor the objectives on a periodic basis to see if a change of direction is needed. The quality objectives must be communicated to the appropriate business organizations to make them aware of interrelated processes they may have to implement and adhere to.

A set of pre-established criteria should indicate what "success" or "completed with full satisfaction" looks like. After all, if you don't know where you are going but continue to walk, you will eventually reach someplace — but not necessarily the place where you intended to go when you started out. Similarly, if the organization does not establish success measures (metrics) for its quality objectives upfront, it will not be able to continue the journey that eventually results in quality products and services, which in turn lead to satisfied customers and world-class quality.

Without an effective communication system to convey quality objectives, even the most sincere efforts to build a results-oriented QMS can fall short, with damaging effects on employee morale and productivity then ensuing and having an adverse impact on the overall image of your organization. The importance of establishing common quality objectives at every level of the organization cannot be understated.

Lack of communication negatively affects employee morale and results in a decline in efficiency. When it fails to establish a dedicated, effective internal communication program on quality objectives, an organization allows its employees to determine and depend on the information (or disinformation) communicated to employees through the grapevine! The dynamics of the workplace can be changed by better managing communications. Notably, the ever-changing methods of communication channels, such as bulletin boards, social media, emails, instant messages, and social media communities, can be exploited to create special opportunities.

Consistent monitoring and measurement allow you to understand the processes that are working within the organization and to identify opportunities for improvement. Of course, without appropriate measures, it is can be difficult to notice improvements. Consequently, performance measures are recognized as an important element of all QMS. Individuals directing the efforts of an organization have a responsibility to know what to measure, when to measure (schedule), what to do with the results, how to communicate the results, and who should receive them.

When we talk about measurement, a quote attributed to one of the founders of modern science, Archimedes, comes to mind: "To measure is to know." In reality, there is no evidence that this quote was actually uttered by Archimedes; research indicates that the credit for this remark perhaps most appropriately belongs to Lord Kelvin. In any event, the quote is clearly right on the mark: How will you implement improvements, if you don't know where the problems are?

Clause 6.3: Planning of Changes

Based on its metrics and results, your organization may decide to implement changes to its QMS. Making changes to the QMS is a necessity if the goal is continuously improving processes, employees, products, performance, and services. There are several different reasons for making a change, and determining the appropriate type of change necessitates the development of a clear and concise business case for introducing new changes. Creating a business case to identify and describe QMS changes will help explain those changes to your organization and boost stakeholders' confidence in its path.

Reason

Suppose you are going to another country for a 15-day vacation. Think about the time you will spend in planning this trip. You would start with where you want to go, which airline you will use, which time of the year you will travel, where you will stay, what you will see, whether you will rent a car, and many other questions. What is the reason for this planning? Simple enough, you want your trip to be successful! Similarly, companies that spend time in planning intend to have a successful QMS and are aware that if they do not use a planned approach to apply changes to their QMS, they will pay more and yet achieve less in the important area of customer satisfaction and contentment.

When they don't appreciate the effects of failing to implement a systematic approach to planning and making appropriate changes when needed, some companies have lost faith in the proper functioning of the QMS and have decided not to pursue it further. The results have been unhappy: more customer and market-share losses, accompanied by significant profit erosion. In contrast, among other collateral benefits, successful implementation of the QMS may result in a greater market share, an increased customer base, positive brand recognition, and a competitive advantage.

Implementation Guidance

To plan for changes, you should identify the problems in the QMS and develop a map of the activities required to make the necessary changes. Interview and gather feedback from all the interested parties who can assist in developing a sound rationale for the change.

Emphasize the reason for the change and decide what needs to be changed. Capture the risks, weaknesses, or potential consequences that you may have identified. Any change in the QMS related to inputs, outputs, availability of resources, identification of risks and opportunities, measurement criteria, metrics, or identification of opportunities for improvement must be evaluated and planned. Consider your business strategy, and ensure that your reasons for making the change are sound and that the change is carried out in a systematic and consistent manner.

Consider all options. Describe which processes and activities will have to be changed, and communicate that understanding widely to obtain feedback and secure trust and confidence. Develop clear goals for the results of the change, associated metrics for each activity, and a timeline (schedule) of when you want these goals to be achieved.

Focus on the availability of resources for the change and the distribution of responsibilities. Develop a clear, detailed business case for the change, one that is easy to communicate and easy to understand by the recipients of the message about the change. This will enable you to develop a vigorous action plan, one that succeeds.

8

Clause 7: Support

Clause 7.1: Resources

Quality products and service assist the organization in maintaining its customer base, improving customer satisfaction, increasing customer loyalty, and reducing the risk and cost of replacing nonconforming products and services. The basic business model for most organizations is to develop products or services and to make a profit by selling them to potential customers. The customers have certain quality expectations when they buy these products and services; if these expectations are not met, the business has to face negative consequences. For all these reasons, a quality management system (QMS) is important for the business, as it addresses these issues and activities.

As your organization begins to concentrate on a formal company-wide QMS, the availability of adequate resources becomes essential to carry out the required activities for developing, implementing, maintaining, and continuously improving the QMS. These resources may include staffing, buildings, tools, hardware, or software. Over time, the provision of the proper resources becomes a necessity to facilitate effective and successful implementation of the QMS.

Many of the operations performed directly impact the salability of products and services. In turn, the quality policy provides guidance throughout the organization as to how those products and services should be provided to customers. Because this policy affects everyone in the organization, all individuals need to be aware of it and the associated quality objectives.

As far as staffing is concerned, necessary skills are required to support the QMS. In some cases, you may find that your organization does not have the expertise needed to develop, sell, and support a product or service. If so, appropriate training must be provided or experienced staff hired. Also, because of constant business-, product-, and services-related fluctuations, the need to have adequate training has emerged as a key consideration for controlling an organization's quality performance. In addition to having qualified individuals to do the assigned jobs, you need to have staff with experience, competence, and the knowledge of how their work affects the quality of the organization's products or services, either positively or negatively.

Every organization engages in communication with its employees regarding topics such as the progress of the company, shareholder/customer expectations, financial and competitive performance, and market share. Such information, along with useful information about quality, must be communicated throughout the company in a deliberate and systematic way, using the most effective communication methods.

Reason

Quality is an important differentiating factor in the ever more competitive global marketplace. Indeed, a product recall due to a failure or poor quality can create negative publicity and damage the organization's reputation.

Organizational knowledge is the process of enhancing the skills, capabilities, and expertise of employees for doing a particular job. Training is crucial for organizational development and success. Employees will be more efficient and productive if they are continuously trained based on company trends and current procedures in the jobs they are performing. This ongoing updating of employees' skill can benefit both your organization and the employees it has hired. Conversely, if they do not have the proper expertise or training in the effectiveness of quality-oriented skills and tools, employees will remain unaware of the possible benefits that these skills and tools can provide in regard to their own responsibilities. Managers tend to give assignments to persons who have demonstrated the ability to achieve goals; in contrast, they tend not to give new assignments to individuals with mediocre performance. This type of favoritism can have significant effects on all employee morale.

Lack of effective communication has led to many customer problems. Consistent outside communication related to quality issues are important for customers who must determine whether any actions are required on their part, such as sending the product back to the company or obtaining guidance from the company to determine the next steps for dealing with the faulty product or service. Communication, when appropriately used, can result in increased customer satisfaction, reduction in wasted time, faster resolution of customer problems, and enhanced understanding of the benefits of the QMS by the staff.

Statutory and regulatory requirements are critical for your organization to understand if it must address these requirements in its products or service. If these requirements are not embedded as product outputs, depending on the requirements and the country, you may not be able to sell the product or service to government agencies or in countries that have made the statutory or regulatory requirements mandatory.

To keep pace in an increasingly competitive world, your business needs to operate as efficiently as possible. To do so, it is essential to maintain the environment needed to execute the processes that will yield the maximum product, process, and operating efficiency. Such an environment can be physical (e.g., buildings) or psychological (e.g., encouraging employees and holding them accountable for adhering to the pre-established processes, with adequate associated schedules).

A structure is required, including adequate buildings and associated utilities needed for the company to grow and be profitable. A well-planned structure helps to reduce unproductive travel time by making transportation more efficient. All too often, time spent by employees on the road is time lost. Designing an organizational infrastructure replete with appropriate equipment, hardware, and software to run the business, adequate transportation, and comprehensive information technology contributes to the organization's overall success and the conformity of its products and services.

The process of replacing obsolete hardware can interrupt your employees' workflow and bring the office to a standstill. You can minimize such disruptions by carefully determining short- and long-term business objectives and deploying technology to produce the intended results.

For every project in your organization, there needs to be an associated, qualified and experienced individual to handle it. Similarly, individuals who are selected for monitoring and measuring of compliance of products or services must have the requisite knowledge and expertise to do the job.

If records of measurement and traceability are required by your customer or are a mandatory statuary or regulatory requirement, it is essential to keep records ("documented information") of calibration of the equipment or devices used. These records serve as proof of the due diligence of your company in ensuring conformity of the product, and they can be used as evidence if necessary in legal actions. The records also validate your obligations in regard to using calibrated equipment.

Implementation Guidance

The leaders of your organization must evaluate the knowledge and skills required to perform various functions to ensure the quality and robustness of the products and services that the company offers. Two types of knowledge are necessary: organizational knowledge and individual knowledge.

Organizational knowledge is obtained by learning about the organization's policies and procedures, reviewing customer feedback, analyzing data obtained from other media (e.g., Twitter, Facebook), studying lessons learned from previous projects, and training the staff to use these lessons learned in subsequent projects to avoid similar mistakes from reoccurring. It also entails learning about the organization's products and understanding the related industry/regulatory requirements.

Individual knowledge can be defined as competence. It is covered in more depth in the discussion of clause 7.2.

The proliferation of quality-oriented activities has also given rise to more types of competence required to do employees' jobs. Dr. W. Edwards Deming emphasized providing training on the job to keep employees' skills current, and it has been proven time and again that employees perform better if they are trained to be aware of the effects of their job performance on other activities in the company or on the performance of the product or service. Continual education creates an atmosphere that encourages individuals to think of new ideas and discover innovative ways to change existing processes to be more efficient. Ongoing training also helps to "sharpen" skill sets and refreshes employee talents by introducing workers to new state-of-the-art tools or techniques and by exposing them to industry best practices and guidelines to implement these practices.

In the face of changing technology and diversified needs of businesses, managers must focus on acquiring the right talent, retaining this pool of talent, and ensuring that these employees' knowledge remains relevant by encouraging them to take required training. Gap analysis of existing talents will show you how your employees' skills overlap and interact, where deficiencies exist, and where opportunities can be realized by offering additional training.

Perhaps the most important aspect of a QMS is the quality policy and accompanying quality objectives that indicate what is supposed to be done and what the company is trying to achieve. A well-communicated policy makes the quality goals and objectives clear to the employees, showing them what is important and what they should be doing to meet these goals. For the QMS to yield consistent results, it is also critical to standardize how processes should be carried out.

To raise the quality bar and heighten awareness of the collateral damage caused by failure to adhere to the QMS requirements, the following points should be emphasized:

- Understanding of the policy and relevant quality objectives
- Making quality objectives and related activities an integral part of each job to support meeting customer requirements
- Keeping key metrics of product and service characteristics, conducting root-cause analysis of the nonconformances, and implementing adequate processes to eliminate the causes of these discontinuities
- Focusing on continual improvement and making employees aware of the positive or adverse effects of individual work performance on overall product or service
- Ensuring continuous training

It is essential to keep the flow of communication open between the leaders and the staff. To create an effective communication system, you may want to develop a regular communication plan that addresses the points shown in Figure 8.1. Where metrics are required as an evidence of conformity, adequate documented information must be retained. There are certain instances where measurement traceability is a mandatory requirement or customer expectation. In these cases the device(s) used to measure must be calibrated for suitability and accuracy. Once again, the records of calibration must be maintained.

1.	The type of information regarding the quality system that you would share with your employees
2.	How often this communication will take place
3.	Who will receive the information
4.	The media by which the information will be shared, for example Video on Demand (VoD), web letter, company meeting, all-hands meeting, a newsletter to employees, etc.
5.	How you will ensure that the communication is taking place according to the plan

Figure 8.1 *Communication Plan*

Clause 7.2: Competence

Competence may be defined as the combination of measurable skills, experience, knowledge, and behaviors that an employee requires to perform on the job. Competence predicts how well an employee will perform on the job. High-caliber, highly competent individuals can help guarantee the organization has an effectively managed, high-quality, and productive workforce at all times.

Reason

Lack of competence impacts customers—indeed, all interested parties who must endure additional expense and irritation when the company's products or services do not meet the stated requirements. These errors may not significantly affect the company's financial numbers, but they may damage its brand and image. If a recall of a product is necessary, however, it may take years for the company to recover from the financial damage and rebuild goodwill with its customers. Conversely, high-quality products and services, created by competent staff, contribute to the profitability and long-term longevity of a company by enabling the firm to charge higher prices for those products or services.

Implementation Guidance

Evaluate which training is appropriate and required, and analyze whether the job can be performed by existing employees with the additional training or whether it will be more cost-efficient to outsource the job to a qualified third party. If you opt to train the existing staff, measure the effectiveness of the training to ensure that it will enable the staff to perform the activities with the desired results.

When bringing in new employees, hire individuals based on competence and education. Retain information related to their previous experience, work performed in previous jobs, and any other documentation that you deem appropriate that positively reflects the capabilities of the individuals.

Clause 7.3: Awareness

Whether new employees are hired or existing employees are retrained, they must be aware of the elements identified in Figure 8.2 on the next page.

Reason

Job-related competence empowers individuals to perform their work to the best of their abilities and ensure customer requirements are met. Competence enables employees to do the job faster and with quality because they know what to do, how to do it, and which results to expect.

The employees who have an edge over other employees are the ones with solid core competencies. These competencies can help an organization to become "best in class."

Implementation Guidance

Many companies have implemented one-month orientation training programs for new employees. During this period, the new hire goes through basic training in policies, processes, and standards. This is a good way to familiarize new employees with the organization's existing culture and process requirements. Subsequently, ongoing refresher training for all employees is required as business necessities change.

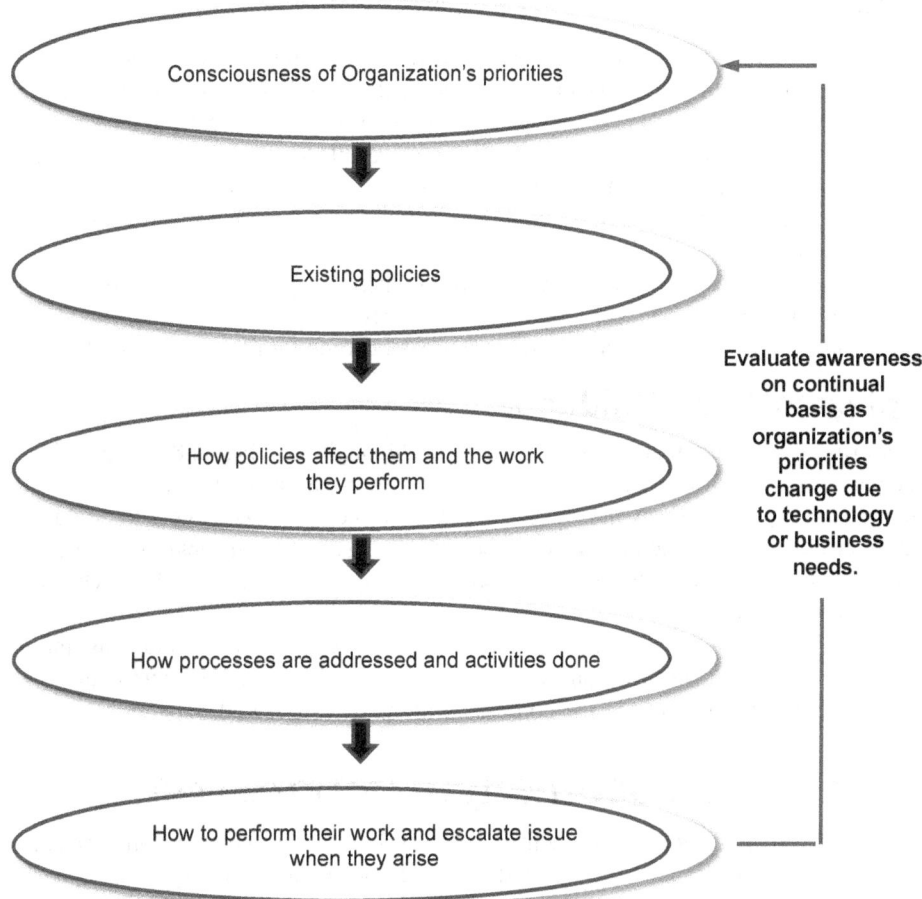

Consciousness of Organization's priorities

Existing policies

How policies affect them and the work they perform

How processes are addressed and activities done

How to perform their work and escalate issue when they arise

Evaluate awareness on continual basis as organization's priorities change due to technology or business needs.

Figure 8.2 *Awareness Steps*

Clause 7.4: Communication

Effective communication to staff, partners, customers, and others—as appropriate—is a fundamental part of the business world. It provides an essential link between the people who make up an organization and others who will be impacted by the message.

Reason

The purpose of having a structured approach to communication is to manage customer expectations and satisfaction. If the customer base is kept well informed on issues that affect users of the company's products and services, it prevents misunderstandings among all parties and the organization. When organizations are able to communicate efficiently both internally and externally, misunderstandings can be resolved in an amicable manner. Furthermore, unnecessary friction is avoided, so that the organization is able to concentrate better on its business.

Acquisition integration has become common when companies acquire other companies for their technology, products, skills, or resources. In this case, you also need to ensure that the newly acquired employees become familiar with your QMS.

Implementation Guidance

Develop a communication plan based on the points highlighted in Figure 8.1, and decide what your organization wants to accomplish with the information it generates. In the communication plan, you may list objectives as well as the tools you will use to produce communications (e.g., social media, email, newspaper ads, or other means). Also describe which information you want to share, how often this communication will take place, and how it will be distributed.

Identify the people in the organization who will be responsible for building and managing the store of information to be communicated. Detailed communication plans also list where records of the communications will be stored.

Clause 7.5: Documented Information

ISO 9001:2015 uses the term "documented information" to refer to both documents and records. Although it does not specify any documented procedures as being required, it does refer to requirements for documented information in some instances. The extent of the documented information depends on the individual organization, including its size, the complexity of the products or services it offers, and the competence of its people.

Reason

As mentioned earlier, ISO 9001:2015 uses the term "documented information" as a requirement for compliance to certain clauses and as records. For example, a component of internal audits compliance is maintaining documented information of audit results—in other words, records.

The word "control" implies that the documented information should be the latest revision and consists of current information that is relevant, usable, and protected. Therefore, document control should ensure that only authorized individuals are able to change controlled documents, and should disallow unauthorized access and unnecessary, non-value-added changes to these documents. Well-planned and well-orchestrated control of documents will prevent compromising of data by unwanted alterations and will limit the damage incurred due to privacy and security breaches.

Controlling documented information supports the majority of the company's activities and saves time when a particular document needs to be retrieved. Without document control, it can be difficult to retrieve a document; indeed, employees may spend hours trying to find the right document.

You may also have difficulty in providing evidence that the company is meeting the QMS requirements without proper controlled internal audit documents during reviews by third-party external auditors.

Implementation Guidance

The term "documented information," according to ISO's definition, refers to information that must be controlled and maintained. Therefore, whenever ISO 9001:2015 uses this term, you are expected to control and maintain documented information—for example, on scope (clause 4.3), the quality policy (clause 5.2), quality objectives (clause 6.2), and confirmation of design and development compliance with the requirements, evidence of the audit program, and results (clause 9.2). Depending on the size of the organization and the products and services that it sells, you can adjust the documented information that is collected and retained to ensure the effectiveness of your QMS.

Although you can use any form of media for documentation, the following elements are standard practice:

- Title of the document
- Date it was created
- Name of the author who created it
- Document number

Industry best practices are techniques or methodologies that, through experience, have been proven to give the desired, constant results. With this definition in mind, it is a best practice to keep a revision history for each document to indicate when the document was changed, who changed it, what was changed, and who reviewed the change. This information may prove extremely valuable in the future for traceability purposes.

A controlled document must be reviewed. That is, each time it is revised, it must be reviewed and receive appropriate approvals to ensure that the content of the document is valid and adequate.

In addition, document control helps in ensuring information security by defining the rules for storing, accessing, formatting, and updating documents. It also indicates who has read/write authority and who can modify the content of a document.

Modification history is required for document control purposes. This history provides for traceability of changes, through information such as when the document was last modified, who modified it, what was modified, why it was modified, and who reviewed the modifications.

To support document control, you can implement a policy that when a document is created, the following steps must be taken:

- Identify future dates when a periodic review of the document will be conducted to evaluate the continuous validity of its content
- Identify the retention period for the document
- Identify the method that will be used to dispose of the document

Finally, in today's world of rapid communication, technology such as social media allows for the quick exchange of both favorable and unfavorable opinions among your customers and prospects. This reality is a major reason to ensure that you stay several steps ahead in meeting your customers' expectations and providing them with world-class products and services by emphasizing the various support activities discussed in this chapter.

9

Clause 8: Operation

Clause 8.1: Operation Planning and Control

When "operation planning" is talked about, it is important to understand the difference between two commonly used plans—that is, strategic and operational. The strategic plan generally sets goals and objectives, identifying a set of strategies to follow for the organization to achieve pre-established goals. It serves as a guide for management that reflects the priorities of the internal stakeholders, but does not contain detailed activity description.

By comparison, the operational plan requires various cross-functional leaders to work together to design the vision, strategies, and related activities such as processes, customer requirements, controlling of outsourced processes, and compliance of products and services with the original requirements. These activities expose areas where support is required.

The operational plan consists of the three W's and quantifies the needs. That is, it answers questions about what, who, when, and how much is needed:

- **What:** addresses the strategies and activities to be conducted
- **Who:** the accountable individual who is charged with accomplishing the activity
- **When:** a schedule indicating when the activities are to be addressed and completed
- **Needs:** identifies the processes, resources, and controls that exist to complete each activity

The operational plan is a tool for management, which uses it to accomplish the following :

- Facilitate the coordination of human and financial resources
- Achieve the organization's goals and objectives
- Confirm that requirements and acceptance criteria have been met

- Validate that appropriate processes are implemented and adhered to
- Ratify that controls are in place for implementing changes and outsourced processes
- Ensure that necessary documentation is maintained

Table 9.1 explains the differences between strategic and operational plans.

Table 9.1 *Strategic versus Operational Plans*

Strategic	Operational
A guidance document for management planning purposes	A customized plan developed for utilization of the organization's resources to accomplish what is identified in the strategic plan
Identifies three to five years' goals that address the strategies	Addresses day-to-day activities that are related to the strategies
Once the strategic plan is developed, minimal changes are made to it.	The operational plan differs from one year to the next.

Reason

Sometimes, functional leads and supervisors are very clear about what they need and want. Often, however, an in-depth analysis must be undertaken of the projects that need to be addressed, the validation of products and services, ways to ensure the requirements are met according to customer expectations, resources required, and the timeline during which the projects have to be completed. This exercise may result in the evaluation of current processes, resources, skills required for the projects, experience and strengths of resources, and needs and demands for building the needed strengths for sustainability.

Operation planning addresses detailed information specifically required to control and direct people to perform the day-to-day activities while adhering to the processes, ensuring the processes are yielding positive results, achieving customer satisfaction based on meeting their requirements, and running the organization. Indeed, the staff frequently refers to the operational plan to accomplish their daily work. In short, the purpose of the operational plan is to provide the staff with a clear and concise picture of their activities, responsibilities, and accountability in harmony with the existing processes—that is, with the goals of the strategic plan.

Operational control relates to the required and committed costs that are associated with an activity. If an activity results in excess capacity, operational control specifies how and where this excess capacity can be utilized. Equally significant, it facilitates the following activities:

- Measurement of the customer experience
- Recognition of the financial implications of the resource allocation decisions for the activities that are outlined in the operational plan
- Decision making regarding whether any of the existing processes need to be changed

As the operational plan is implemented, operational control is used to ensure that results are achieved in an efficient and effective manner. This "controlling" aspect relies on knowledge of problematic areas of your organization's operations and identification of areas where changes are required to improve operational efficiency.

Control and operation planning are necessary to confirm that day-to-day actions are consistent with established strategies and goals and that the organization's product or service has met customer requirements. It requires maintaining a focus on events in a given period. If those results have not met the intended purpose and the performance does not meet required standards, planned changes must be made. Such action may involve retraining staff in maintaining necessary documentation, redesigning the processes, providing overall process-related training to the staff, or emphasizing acceptance criteria.

Implementation Guidance

To ensure coordinated efforts in operation planning, it is very important to implement the following steps:

- Align key stakeholders from the start.
- Ensure everyone has a thorough understanding of the "big" picture and related processes and acceptance criteria.
- Obtain concurrence on roles, responsibilities, and timelines.
- Map out interactions between functional organizations to accomplish certain activities.
- Take an inventory of all resources—human, financial and physical, such as buildings, rooms, and spaces.
- Ensure that the definition of compliance in regard to the organization's products and services is clearly understood.
- Implement the necessary control to avoid unintended changes to the operational plan.

The initial step in the control process is to identify what will necessitate a change and when it will occur. Generally, managers identify vision, strategies, and mission as the areas requiring control during their planning process. In deciding how to control unintended changes, top management must provide training on the impact of changes, which can relate to financial concerns, resources, or customer satisfaction. Those changes that need to be addressed must be carefully identified and selected based on their strategic value and impact. This can be accomplished by developing a customer and business importance weighting system, in which the changes that are assessed as having a high impact are implemented first.

Establishing a change control board (CCB) to conduct analysis of the change effect is a good way to conduct a systematic evaluation. The membership of the CCB might then consist of experienced employees who are called upon each time a change is introduced. This team can then assess what needs to be done to address a given change and develop a complete analysis of the impact to enable proper decision making.

Clause 8.2: Requirements for Products and Services

Clause 8.2.1: Customer Communication

A great idea for a product that you think will capture consumers' attention and address a desperate need may not, in fact, be the right product! We have seen organizations push products out the door that have been developed in "silos" due to internal competition or because managers are convinced that what they are about to sell is perfect. Leaving the customer completely out of the development loop is not a good idea. No matter how good your product or service is, you will have a hard time convincing anyone to buy it if you fail to provide proper information regarding that product or service or do not handle customer inquiries in a systematic and timely manner.

The current globalization of trade, which has increased both domestic and international trade pressures, has also brought new demands to interact with customers more extensively and to more fully understand their requirements of the product or service, including related industry and regulatory requirements. It is more important than ever to review customer requirements up front to confirm the organization's ability to meet those requirements in its products and services. Such a review necessitates the participation of and collaboration with the affected stakeholders in your organization.

Knowledge and understanding of your customers' needs is a crucial element for ensuring a successful business, especially when certain requirements are not specified by your customers but are absolutely mandatory for the use of your product or service. To be successful, companies must thoroughly research their customers and their stated needs, including requirements for release, distribution, and post-delivery activities.

Reason

No business can succeed without understanding its customers, its products and services, and the customer requirements in general. Moreover, research has shown that requirement defects are the most difficult and costly errors to fix once they spread to the subsequent phases of design and then into the final product.

Today's communication techniques have dramatically changed from those of the past. New technologies are being used for communication and interaction among the general population; contact through social media, online interactions, blogs, Tweets, mobile devices, and means is becoming commonplace. These technologies are also changing the way companies interact with their customers.

At the same time, business competition is growing ever more fierce. Trying to develop products without applying rigor when collecting requirements, understanding what is needed by the customer, knowing customer pain-points, developing proper processes to control customer-furnished property, creating contingency actions, and keeping appropriate documentation may give your competitors an advantage over your own organization. Identifying customer needs through research, however, will equip you with the data needed to determine how to keep your customers happy and how to succeed with your product or service. The fact that potential customers are listening to what others say about your products and services needs to be incorporated into your development process, so that customers' requirements and your obligation for meeting those requirements are considered first and foremost.

Review of the requirements prior to committing to supply the product or service will, in the long term, be beneficial to both your organization and the customer for a variety of reasons. Specifically, such a review will:

- Confirm that your organization understands the product and service requirements and related industry and regulatory requirements
- Identify requirements that are needed for the use of the product or service, but that are not explicitly stated by the customer
- Confirm that your organization has the ability to meet the requirements
- Identify any requirements differing from those previously stated
- Enable you to retain documentation on any new requirements

Fixing problems associated with requirements takes the most time and produces the worst consequences. To avoid any future misunderstandings or litigation, it is essential to keep appropriate documentation of any changes to the requirements and to ensure that pertinent individuals within your organization who are affected by those changes are notified of the changes.

Implementation Guidance: Clauses 8.1–8.2.4

Bad requirements may result in unhappy customers, derogatory effects on your company "brand," lawsuits, cost overruns, schedule slips, overworked employees, and lost profitability. In your product or service development life cycle, you should pay extra attention to the key activities related to the requirements:

- Consider whether your organization can meet the requirements.
- Identify requirements that are mandatory for the use of the product or service but are not included in the requirements.
- Understand related industry and regulatory requirements.
- Identify and understand delivery and post-delivery requirements.
- Identify and resolve any contract or order requirements not stated previously.
- Identify any outsourced processes and ensure that they adhere to the appropriate quality standards, specifically, yours!
- Conduct a review of the requirements.
- Keep detailed minutes of the requirements review.
- Control new changes by documenting and evaluating the impact of each change.
- Keep documented details of any changes.
- In the event there are no written requirements from the customer, confirm the requirements with the customer before proceeding.

It might seem obvious, but have you looked at your company's customer communication process and handling of customer documentation of physical property? If not, now may be the right time to do so. Emphasize the following issues in this review:

- Providing detailed information regarding your products or services to the customer
- Establishing a systematic way to receive, document, and address customer inquiries, complaints, and feedback
- Developing a process for handling or controlling any property that belongs to the customer

We have seen many companies establish a customer listening program, taking required actions and keeping a customer-first perspective in their decision making. There are several ways to implement a customer listening program and interact with customers in a positive way:

- Performing telephone or face-to-face interviews. Face-to-face interviews can yield great results, but they are expensive, especially if you have to travel to conduct these interviews. Telephone interviews are equally effective in gathering data, provided you are able to hold the respondent's interest in the telephone interview long enough for it to be completed before the individual at the other end decides to "hang up"!

- Administering a simple, easy-to-understand questionnaire, either by mail or online.
- Administering a clear and concise survey, either by mail or online. If you offer a small incentive for the completion of the survey, you may see better results in the responses.
- Conducting user or focus groups, where you can mingle with customers or potential customers and obtain live feedback.

The art of asking the right questions to get constructive, useful information for your products or service is more complicated than many people appreciate. Without the right type of questions, you will not be able to obtain the data you need for implementing corrective actions. Ideally, you should develop a list of questions that are easy to understand and whose answers can provide you with important facts to act upon. After developing the questionnaire, determine how the data obtained for each of the questions might be used. This exercise may suggest which questions need fine-tuning or need to be replaced with others that will give you additional insights from the customer.

Following are a few key questions that you may want to include in your interviews:

- What do you consider when purchasing this product or service?
- What do you like or dislike about the products or services currently on the market?
- Which vendor do you currently use for the product or service?
- Which aspects of the product or service are working or not working for you?
- What would you say are your main frustrations?
- Which areas would you suggest for improvement?
- Does this sound like something that can solve your problems and address your frustrations?

Today, email interaction is probably the most widely used method to obtain customer feedback. If you decide to apply this method, be careful not to send too many emails, to the point that your customers start to ignore your messages by diverting them directly to their "junk "mailbox or clicking "unsubscribe." Investigate who in your organization is sending emails to the same customers to avoid bombarding recipients with too many messages from the same company. Emphasize knowing the right individual to receive the email to obtain the information you require.

Blogs, newsletters, and the use of social media are all good ways to communicate with customers and engage with them to identify enhancement ideas and opportunities to improve, and to determine what is and what is not working for them.

One of the most effective and inexpensive ways to interact with your customers is through user group meetings, where customers may feel more comfortable in discussing new ideas, describing any competing products they may have seen or used, and providing data on product functionalities causing them to struggle.

Actions are stronger than words! When you are communicating and obtaining information from your customers and engaging them on a regular basis to develop requirements, your goal should be to improve your products based on their feedback and to increase both your market share and your customers' loyalty. Nurturing interactions with customers on an ongoing basis and establishing a genuine relationship will naturally make a major impact on your market share and customer satisfaction levels.

Clause 8.3: Design and Development of Products and Services

In today's technology-driven world, the importance of product design and development is growing. Organizations are now required to design and develop faster and more efficiently. This has increased the importance of establishing, implementing, and maintaining a consistent process for these activities. The resulting "life cycle" includes different phases and specifies the order in which those phases are executed. Each phase in this life cycle produces a deliverable required by the next phase. The most commonly used phases are (1) analyze, (2) gather requirements, (3) develop a design, and (4) build a product or a service. Within each phase, multiple steps must be addressed before moving on to the subsequent phase. This process is applicable to enhancements to an existing product or service, extensions of a product or service with additional functionality, and introduction of new lines and new-to-the-world innovations.

In this section, we will address design and development only. All mature and successful companies are more likely to have some type of design and development process. Although design and development are often perceived as a creative process, they actually represent a planned process that involves specific inputs, outputs, documentation, and steps. This approach has multiple benefits:

- It facilitates a consistent decision-making process.
- It ensures that all pertinent steps are discussed and addressed.
- It opens up cross-functional communication channels.

To develop a robust product or service that meets customer requirements, during planning, emphasis is given to various activities such as reviews, verification and validation, interaction between individuals involved, and involvement of customers to gather feedback. In addition, all inputs are considered, and outputs are identified along with the process for handling changes and conducting reviews.

Reason

The activities carried out when choosing the look and feel of the product or service, selecting processes, and examining the entire architecture or infrastructure are collectively referred to as *design*. The entire process of analyzing return on investment, assessing marketing opportunities, capturing the right customer requirements, identifying inputs and outputs, and creating, validating, and modifying the product or service is referred to as *development*. Both design and development are more important today than ever because customers are demanding higher quality and are switching rapidly to other companies that can deliver the quality they expect. In this fast-paced environment, design and development ceases to be an ad hoc, sporadic activity and becomes a well-defined action. For companies operating in this milieu, problems, delays, and mixed-up design and development activities can easily shift from being an annoyance to being revenue and brand threatening.

Popular products and services are not simply designed in one fell swoop, but rather go through iterations of analysis, design studies, testing, modifying, and retesting until they are perfected. Indeed, successful companies spend astounding amounts of time and money in designing and developing their products. Development is normally done by a project team, many times utilizing both internal and external resources in the process. In very few cases are products and services developed by single individuals working in silos. As part of its work, the project team develops estimates that are utilized to forecast a selling price and potential profit for the company.

Design and development drive organizational success because they directly and significantly impact nearly all of the critical determinants for success. Design and development can also be a key means of coordinating an organization's activities with its supply chain members. If your organization is outsourcing some of its design/development steps, you may be able to request that your suppliers participate in design reviews, which are essential mechanisms for communication and coordination of the flow of information, and for safeguarding cost-effective and timely designs and development.

The processes of developing new products or services differ from company to company, and even within the same company. However, irrespective of any organizational differences, a good product is always the outcome of the most important parameters of systematic design and development effort, including well-defined planning, requirements gathering, identifying proper inputs and outputs, testing, and controlling changes. Considerations and decisions taken during the design and development phases, and the subsequent testing of those elements, will determine the extent to which the activity has helped or hindered the company's quest for sustainability.

Implementation Guidance

There is a growing realization today that a company that can design and develop a product or service faster than its competition can get to the market first and enjoy a unique competitive advantage. This is true not only because the life cycle is shorter for the first-to-market organization, but also often because of factors related to robust features, performance, quality, and cost. To address all of these elements, emphasis must be placed on features, performance, quality and cost during many activities in the life cycle. Figure 9.1 depicts the key elements that you must consider during design and development of a product or service.

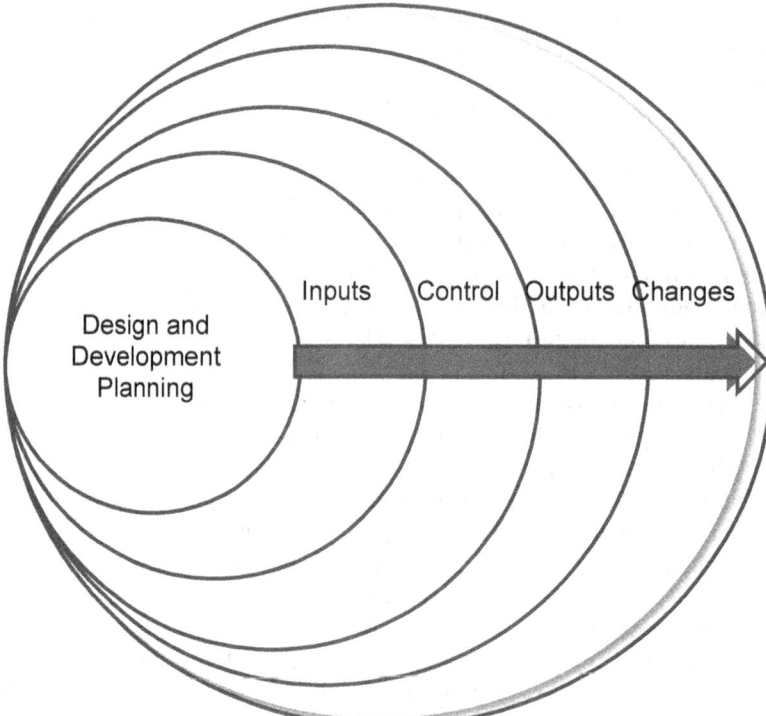

Figure 9.1 *Design and Development Considerations*

Design and Development Planning

Considerations for planning should include the following:

- Evaluating the complexity of design and development activities, and estimating time they will take

- Conducting reviews
- Identifying who will be responsible and accountable
- Performing verification and validation activities
- Identifying inside or outside resources
- Obtaining feedback by involving customers and users
- Obtaining requirements for successive products or services
- Documenting evidence to show the requirements are met

Design and Development Inputs

Considerations related to inputs should include these factors:

- Addressing functional requirements, including performance, industry and regulatory requirements, and standards or practices the organization has agreed to adhere to
- Information achieved from similar previous products and services
- Impacts and implications of failures
- Resolution of conflicting inputs

Design and Development Controls

Considerations for controls should include these issues:
- Definition of the results to be obtained
- Conducting reviews to evaluate whether requirements have been met and identifying actions needed to address any problems uncovered
- Verification activities conducted to ensure outputs meet the input requirements and validation activities conducted to ensure requirements have been met
- Documented evidence of these activities being carried out

Design and Development Outputs

Considerations for outputs should include the following:
- The outputs must meet the input requirements and indicate the characteristics of the intended purpose.
- The outputs are suitable for successive products and services.

Design and Development Changes

Considerations for changes should include these issues:
- Documented change control history identifying authorizations, impacts, reviews, and minutes

Clause 8.4: Control of Externally Provided Processes, Products, and Services

Top-performing organizations don't just reduce costs in design and development, but do so in a manner that adds value to the business. Some of these organizations have learned that one of their most valuable tools in achieving this dual aim is outsourcing their processes, products, and services. Rather than performing the work within its own facilities, the company uses an outside supplier after evaluating the return on investment from such outsourcing. The main reason for implementing this approach is cost savings or better cost control over the outsourced function.

The popularity of outsourcing has grown due to a change in business philosophy. In the early 1970s and 1980s, many companies acquired other companies to increase their inventory of offered products and services. Such acquisitions often caused product and resource integration challenges. In turn, companies began to look for competencies and expertise that would provide a competitive advantage by farming out—outsourcing—certain activities and functions. Successful outsourcing requires strong understanding of the processes and controls that need to be established as part of this relationship. For startup companies, outsourcing is an attractive option because it can free the entrepreneur from mandated but time-consuming tasks, instead allowing the entrepreneur to concentrate on revenue-generating ideas. Of course, there are also potential disadvantages associated with outsourcing, such as poor quality control, inability of the outsourced company to understand industry and regulatory requirements, lack of design and development processes, inadequate and inexperienced resources, and low emphasis on validation activities.

Reason

An outsourced process is a process that you have identified as required for your internal quality management system and that you have decided to give to an external party (a supplier) to address. This process is not under the umbrella of your own internal quality management system. Settling details of the expected standards, schedules, accountability, and legal compliance requirements will help to clarify your expectations of the supplier.

Failure to establish a proper outsourcing process and control between your company and the supplier regarding your conditions to meet the requirements of your quality management system can lead to a lengthy bid process, poor results, increased costs, and loss of strategic alignment. In contrast, a clear understanding between your organization and the supplier will confirm the roles and responsibilities of both parties, which is beneficial when it comes to monitoring the relationship's success. The controls established as part of the agreement can also reveal whether a supplier's performance is falling short or deteriorating. A contract, as a means of establishing control between a company and its supplier, can be a vital piece of evidence if the relationship experiences problems and litigation becomes necessary..

Implementation Guidance

Companies usually outsource activities to a vendor that specializes in a given function and performs that function more efficiently than the company could. Once you have made the decision to outsource, you need to consider a number of factors that will influence the success of the relationship to result in robust products and services. In the scope of your QMS, include all outsourced processes affecting the product and service quality.

You must consider a number of issues in making a successful transition to outsourcing and in forming a partner relationship with the supplier. The nature of control will depend on the experience and reputation of the supplier, the importance of the outsourced process, and the risk involved to your organization. If you already have the competence and expertise needed to carry out the outsourced activity, then you undoubtedly have already identified the necessary process control activities. In such a case, it will be easy for you to include these control activities in the contract with the supplier. If you do not have these activities specified, and the supplier has its own process, you will have to review this process and include any additional requirements you may have; you will also have to obtain necessary evidence of compliance with your requirements from the supplier of the outsourced activity. You may be able to verify the output from the outsourced process by subsequent monitoring or measurement.

Following are some guidelines for controlling outsourced processes, where you are using your suppliers to directly provide products or services to your customers:

- Provide the supplier with your quality manual, reflecting the processes that must be adhered to.
- Specify detailed requirements for processes, products, and services that you wish the supplier to address, along with measurable output criteria and any essential industry and regulatory requirements. Communicate the required qualifications and expertise needed, including the validation activities you plan to conduct and your acceptance criteria on your purchase order.
- Include detailed requirements in the supplier contract.
- If the supplier has its own quality manual, review it and identify any gaps on the activities you require; include these requirements in the contract.
- Conduct audits of the supplier's QMS and its adherence to the pre-established processes.
- Conduct incoming inspections to limit your risks.

Clause 8.5: Production and Service Provision

In this section, we clarify the difference between the design process and the production and service provision. The latter involves those processes that are repeatedly used to generate a product or to deliver a service. Production and service provision differs from the design process in that it is organized to reproduce a product or service to the same standard every time. By comparison, the design process is a creative process requiring certain controls to meet established objectives, while the production process requires controls for required standards. The emphasis in production and service provision is on controlling the product and all essential steps of the production process, which are planned and conducted under controlled conditions, to ensure customer requirements are met.

Planning must be done for all products and services provision and carried out under controlled conditions. Those conditions are defined based on characteristics, availability, and adherence of processes; means to monitor and measure outputs; identification and traceability; and preservation of customer property. The controlled conditions are intended to ensure that the result of the operational process always fulfills the customers' requirements.

Reason

The product or service provision requirements are critical for the entire unified quality system, and the processes need to be carried out and executed under controlled conditions. Emphasis is placed here on the interaction between the "entire" production process rather than on individual, stand-alone processes, as successful operations also include outputs. The sequence in which processes are carried out affects the outputs and ultimately influences the quality, so attention should be given to the sequence of the activities that you address. Attention should also be paid to the entrance and exit criteria of each process to avoid problem workarounds that may result into additional work, cost overruns, and negative effects on customer satisfaction.

Implementation Guidance

You should identify requirements for operations that yield products or deliver services so as to ensure compliance with those requirements and satisfy the needs and expectations of customers. To meet these needs and expectations, the following activities are recommended:

- Evaluate the effectiveness of the production or service provision by reviewing all processes and by confirming that related activities are planned and conducted under controlled conditions.

- Ensure that documentation that defines the characteristics of the product is available, with clear work processes for activities and subsequent stages for achieving product conformity according to the acceptance criteria.
- Control all production processes, identifying and showing the interactions of these processes with other related processes and outputs.
- Consider ways to safeguard and protect the outputs.
- Ensure that quality plans address what, how, and when questions, and utilize them to control production and service activities, taking into consideration customer delivery requirements by utilizing competent staff members in this process.
- Measure the effectiveness of production processes in meeting customer requirements by using performance indicators to monitor reduction of variance and improvements in production processes.
- Review and control changes to ensure consistency with requirements. and document minutes of these reviews.
- Emphasize industry and regulatory requirements up front in the design and development phases.
- If required, develop a traceability method for unique identification, and consider post-delivery logistics such as maintenance and warranty provisions.

Clause 8.6: Release of Products and Services

To come to fruition and enhance the company's reputation and coffers, products and services take investment, support, adherence, and a lot of discipline. Good release management practices ensure that when your products and services are launched into the marketplace, they will meet customer requirements, be successfully deployed by satisfied customers, and enable your organization to gain a new customer base.

Reason

Untimely and unplanned release decisions are associated with high costs and may cause potential losses long after they are made. Competitive pressures related to decisions about products and services, time to market, and release timing are important, as are complex considerations related to ensuring acceptance criteria are met and evidence of traceability of release authorization is maintained.

Implementation Guidance

- Establish a set of release criteria, indicating the entrance and exit criteria at different stages of a product or service.
- Provide training to appropriate individuals so they understand the release criteria.
- Retain documented information on the release, indicating the fulfillment of the acceptance criteria.
- Keep traceability logs for those individuals who authorized the release.

Clause 8.7: Control of Nonconforming Outputs

When a product or service does not meet customer requirements, it is considered *nonconformance*. In the event of a nonconformance, a formal procedure is required for storing the nonconforming product or identifying the nonconforming service, finding who has the pertinent responsibilities for the product or service, determining what is to be done, isolating the corrective action to be taken, and finding out who is to be informed.

Reason

To limit your organization's liability and maintain adequate customer satisfaction, a quick response to a nonconforming output is necessary to maintain the company's favorable reputation and limit undesired consequences. This requires a formal approach to identify and separate these outputs to prevent their further distribution and limit liability, thereby maintaining customer satisfaction. Any delays in the containment effort may result in additional costs and negatively affect both customer relationships and market share.

Implementation Guidance

Implement proper controls to identify and prevent further use of nonconforming products or services by isolating them. In addition:

- Notify affected customers.
- Document the following:
  - Description of the nonconformance.
  - The action taken to address it.

- If any customer concessions were obtained. Note that a concession authorization allows you to ship nonconforming output or provide nonconforming service, under controlled conditions. Make sure that you obtain these concessions in writing prior to shipping.
- The individual who made the decision on action related to the nonconformance.
- Check release policies for further processing or shipment of the product or the use of the service.
- Fix and verify conformance to the requirement.

10

Clause 9: Performance Evaluation

The famous quote "To measure is to know" says it all. Once again, we will not go into a deep discussion of whether this quote was said originally by Lord Kelvin and whether the original wording was "When you can measure what you are speaking about, and express it in numbers, you know something about it." The fact remains that if you do not measure, you cannot know if you are meeting your goals. These goals could be related to improving internal business processes, customer satisfaction, the financial bottom line, external communications, time to market, or product quality. Having an understanding of your company's baseline, and where you stand relative to this baseline will help you identify opportunities for improvement. Defining, monitoring, and analyzing data to ensure valid results are achieved will also help your company identify new prospects for product and service innovation.

Customer perceptions are important, of course. All too often, however, we have seen measurement plans implemented for products or services where the measures generate the expected outputs, yet do not help in increasing customer satisfaction. This is a strong indication that measures should be selected carefully to ensure they will bring the intended results.

Business complexity surrounds us, and it is becoming increasingly more difficult to make well-informed decisions on improvements, customer needs, and customer issues. Answering the what, when, where, and why questions through data analysis will enable you to assess how well your quality management system is working and how happy your customers are with your organization's products and services. Careful analysis of data is an important part of every evaluation, and it is done to look for patterns (trends). These patterns can relate to customer satisfaction, product failures, product returns, service complaints, service failures, increase in warranty costs, and many other issues.

With the focus on product evaluation, our descriptions of key performance indicators (KPIs) in Chapter 4 and related tools for comingling traditional management concerns and the concerns of the quality professional now come front and center. Clause 9 is in many respects the point at which the return on investment from the QMS becomes clear to top management.

Clause 9.1: Monitoring, Measurement, Analysis, and Evaluation

No matter how well your business is running, you must recognize that a crowded market with several competing products and services requires your organization to have a strategy to continuously improve to differentiate itself from its competitors. To clarify what sets your product apart from the competition, you need a clearly articulated plan of action—a true process designed to capture and analyze important issues about your product and your customers' perception of its value to them. As discussed earlier, this is your "value proposition."

Isolating areas that need monitoring, along with any related measures, requires a structured approach. You must identify quality issues requiring improvements to move your organization in the right direction. As an example, suppose that your warranty costs are escalating and you would like to control these costs. You can address this situation by taking the following steps:

- Analyzing those products with high warranty costs
- Isolating the reasons for those high costs
- Conducting an analysis of the causes
- Implementing corrective process(es)
- Training appropriate individuals
- Standardizing the process after it is proven to work in bringing down those warranty costs

A systematic approach for monitoring and measuring requires a well-thought-out plan indicating the timing and frequency of the associated activities as well as when the results will be analyzed and evaluated to determine the effectiveness of your quality management system. Care is required to remain objective in regard to the data and information received. Too often, organizations ask all but the right questions of themselves, especially in those areas related to family agreements or the decisions of a revered founder. If the net result is high warranty costs and the root cause is a unilateral decision by an uninformed and operationally distant relative, the data must speak for itself. An opinion that created these losses cannot be simply countered with your own conjecture. Instead, the data must take the lead role in the argument made, and to do that it must be complete, unambiguous, and irrefutable.

Reason

Without an effective monitoring, measurement, and analysis process, you are not able to quantify progress achieved or separate the areas of your business that require attention for further improvement. Monitoring, measurement, and analysis help you in the following areas:

- Isolation of root causes of the problems by analysis of data
- Identification of areas requiring remedial actions
- Evaluation of compliance with industry and regulatory requirements
- Improvement of overall efficiency of the quality management system, thereby increasing customer satisfaction and reducing costs
- Implementation of design or production changes to eliminate further customer dissatisfaction

Now that we have clarified the general importance of monitoring, measurement, and analysis, we can highlight other critical measurement factors that have profound positive effects on customers when data is analyzed and acted upon to fix problems and increase efficiency. Regular measurements of customer satisfaction and quality of your products or service will:

- Provide leading indicators of repeat customer intentions and loyalty
- Decrease negative word-of-mouth communications
- Reduce overall customer changes
- Reduce costs of mitigating problems

In addition, a well-organized and precise monitoring plan will help you:

- Define the activities that need to be performed to monitor, measure, conduct analysis, and gather relevant data
- Evaluate the efficiency of any automated tools you are using to address the activities
- Determine resource requirements for the activities to be addressed
- Obtain data on areas where improvements are required
- Continually improve performance of those issues that are of importance to your customers

Customer satisfaction measures how products or services supplied by your company meet your customer's expectations. Studies show that increased customer satisfaction results in loyal customers who will continue to give your organization repeat business. Satisfied customers will tell their friends about their positive experiences with your products or service, resulting in new customers and more revenues. The opposite effect is far worse: It's often reported that a dissatisfied customer will tell seven or eight more people of their difficulties, and these need not be friends but instead may be "anyone who will listen."

Without clear and precise understanding of what should be measured and how data should be collected, analyzed, and corrected, the company is operating as a rudderless ship. Accumulating data and analysis of customer satisfaction through survey results, one-on-one interviews, user groups, or any other means will increase your understanding of the needs and expectations of your customers; it will enable your organization to change or enhance its current products or services based on these findings, determine whether new products or services should be developed, and identify how well it is doing relative to its competitors. The first step toward success in business is to know exactly what the customer wants. Not partially—exactly. Great companies go to elaborate lengths to learn about their customers' wants and needs, often by observation, user groups, and beta testing.

Implementation Guidance

There should be some connection between monitoring/measuring activities and bottom-line results; otherwise, the program will not get the priority and visibility it needs to succeed. As a part of your ongoing process maintenance, implementing a regular schedule for when and how often you monitor and measure your products, processes, or services will depend on factors such as the size of your organization, business risks, and criticality.

The first step is to determine what you will be monitoring and measuring. For example, if you decide to monitor customer satisfaction, consider different approaches to research your customers' feelings and experiences, including surveys, user groups, and social media. If you decide to send a survey, you must thoughtfully design the questions to get responses that will allow you to take actions. Moreover, questions must be developed with the understanding of the gap between customer expectations and satisfaction. Do not develop a long survey for every aspect of the product or service; just start with simple questions, typically no more than 10, and all easily read and unambiguous.

If your company is to offer reliable products or services, you must capture those metrics that will provide a true picture of where the company stands as far as customer satisfaction and product quality are concerned.

In the service industry, it is tricky to identify relevant measures because customers often vary considerably. Many services are highly customized, leading to unpredictable results for customers. To create repeat customers, the service industry often depends on measures that allow exceptional performance to remain competitive, profitable, and successful. Some of these service measures are summarized here; you should select the measures that best meet your goals and strategies. For example, if your goals are to increase on-time delivery percentage and to reduce the time it takes to fix a customer-found problem, your metric selection should address these issues. Typical service goals include:

- On-time delivery
- Time to fix a problem
- Availability
- Effectiveness

We have also identified some of the most frequently used product measures, which will assist you in identifying the ones that are critical and necessary for your business:

- Mean time between failures
- Time to adoption
- Number of defects
- Warranty claims per product
- Warranty claims as a percentage of sales
- Shipping errors per shipment
- Shipment on-time percentage
- Survey complaints
- Customer satisfaction

Depending on your business needs and problems identified, you will want to select the measures that are most appropriate. Regardless of the product or service provided by your company, you should choose measures that are actionable. A measure is actionable if:

- It can be defined.
- The data can be collected and analyzed.
- The data identifies the gaps.
- The gaps can be addressed by implementation of a process or process improvement.

Of course, if the customer is expecting something different, no matter how well your product or service performs, customer satisfaction will be low. To ensure that you truly understand customer requirements, needs, and expectations, you must determine when and how often you will send surveys to customers. For example, you may want to send a "just in time" survey to the customer right after a product or service is delivered (often called a "transactional" survey), when the experience is still fresh in the customer's mind. Alternatively, you might choose to send a periodic survey to your customers once every six months or once a year that addresses satisfaction with several aspects of your business. Such surveys are often referred to as "relational" surveys.

Collecting the data for the sake of keeping information is simply waste of time and resources. We include this statement because this practice is too often discovered during internal or third-party audits. What may appear as common sense—that is, the effort to capture and then effectively manage customer satisfaction data—presents a real challenge when the quality professional receives pushback from those who question the sample size, the degree of specificity of customers' responses, or the structure and focus of the survey questions. To avoid this outcome, it is imperative to include all those who will likely be affected by results in the survey's development. Make the survey "theirs" before you send it to your customers.

Once the data is collected, successful and best-in-class organizations deploy stringent processes to use the information collected to judge whether any portions of the quality management system needs to be improved. Whether you are collecting data on conformity of products and services, customer satisfaction, effectiveness of the quality management system, results of any corrective actions, or performance of your partners and suppliers, you must understand how you will use the information that is collected, who will analyze and evaluate it, whether you will use tools such as root-cause analysis to identify the causes, and how you will prioritize the actions to be taken.

Have a detailed understanding of the current state of your business in the following areas:

- Customer satisfaction
- Customer complaints
- Product or service problems
- Maintenance/monitoring of the equipment
- Market and competitors

Develop methods to monitor and measure, conduct analysis of data, and evaluate the results to ensure the quality management system is effective. Continue to make adjustments as necessary to keep the competition at bay, your quality standards high, and your company brand associated with a positive image.

Clause 9.2: Internal Audit

The term *internal audit* raises two immediate and negative reactions: Why are we being audited and what have we done wrong? These two reactions can be easily overcome by communicating the benefits of an internal audit to your staff. Let it be known that an internal program assists in monitoring compliance with company processes and regulatory requirements, tests internal control and detects or prevents fraudulent activities. It is a systematic and disciplined approach to improve your organization's effectiveness and manage risks. An internal audit is an efficient tool that creates positive change and harvests the results of improving products and services.

Reason

Sometimes functional teams are very clear about what they have to do to develop a product or offer a service. Verification through an independent and in-depth analysis, however, may be required to ensure customer requirements are met and required processes were truly followed. We have seen examples where managers have identified vision, strategies, and execution as the areas requiring control during the initial planning process, yet the time to market is then given precedence by these same managers, thereby cutting the time for process adherence and validation activities. This contradictory approach often backfires and results in increased product- or service-related issues.

The audit exercise usually results in identifying nonconformances with pre-established processes and the requirements of the quality management system. In addition, the internal audit is—perhaps most importantly from top management's perspective—designed to measure effectiveness through inquiry and comparison of initial planning and projected results against actual performance. For example, a new design might be highly scripted; the initial plan includes a Gantt chart and necessary design features, among many other planned activities. The auditor can use this information to ask the design group if they achieved their target dates and if all the expected features made it into the final product. The answers to these questions provide a window into the effectiveness of the design process, and the auditor can then work with the auditees to explore how and perhaps what to do for the next design to improve performance and process effectiveness.

Implementation Guidance

Depending on the size of your company and the vigor with which you address the improvement program, you may need to assign the internal audit activity to selected, trained individuals. The size of this pool will depend on the company's size and geographic locations, domestic versus global branches, and other factors. One principle to remember is that for the audit program to be effective, no auditor should be auditing his or her own functional area. Individuals cannot audit their own work because they cannot be truly impartial.

The internal audit system may include templates, checklists, or existing process documents that can be used by the auditors. Many companies have online systems to document their audit findings and suggested areas of improvement.

Developing a strategy for the internal audit is an important preliminary step. To ensure a successful audit program, eight critical activities must be considered up front:

- Resources: who will conduct the audits
- Interval/schedule: how often audits will be conducted
- Methodology: how audits will be conducted and what will be the scope of each audit
- Training: how the auditors will be trained and retrained on an as-needed basis
- Audit results: how the audit results will be reported
- Corrective actions: how issues identified during the audits will be addressed
- Responsibility: who will implement remedial actions
- Retention of audit documents: how the documents pertaining to the audit will be retained (stored)

To facilitate an effective audit program, training must be provided to the auditors. Such training should be directed to ensuring consistency between various audits in your organization and increasing the overall proficiency of the auditors. Prior to the actual interviews, studying previous audit results will help the auditor become familiar with any previously discovered nonconformances and the corrective actions designed to address them. While it is important to validate the sustainability of the corrective action implemented, it is also common practice to start a new audit by reviewing previous external third-party audit results or the results of previously conducted internal audits.

Once audits are performed, the results should be reviewed and analyzed. Some observations may be simple to address. Other nonconformances may require corrective actions, including further revision of a process or a service, perhaps training of interested parties, and notifying customers if the change will affect them.

Obtaining feedback from the auditors after the audit is a good way to continuously evolve the audit system and related documents such as checklists, audit reports, and templates. With this approach, the entire audit system becomes a valuable asset to determine if your quality management system is working as intended.

One final note: We encourage you to communicate the difference between an internal audit and an external audit. The internal, or "first-party," audit is conducted by someone just like you: an employee of your company who already possesses a great deal of information and understanding of how things work in your company. The external, or "third-party," auditor is not aware of how things really work deep inside your company; he or she is strictly an independent and (ideally) impartial interpreter of the data encountered during the audit, guided only by the ISO 9001 standard and whatever documented information you provide. Of course, both types of auditors will ask questions and observe activities, but the external auditor is unaware of many things that an employee might know or understand.

Each perspective is important! While the external auditor cannot suggest changes or offer his or her own observations from visiting other companies, the internal auditor is encouraged to suggest and discuss any improvement ideas. After all, the internal auditor has audited many departments in the company and perhaps seen other approaches along the way that could be helpful. This "helpfulness" is strictly not allowed from a third-party auditor because then the auditor's next visit to your operation could, in part, be an audit of his or her own work.

Encourage your fellow employees to work far more closely and openly with your internal audit team—that is, the team made up of their fellow employees. It is far better to conduct a free and open internal audit to ensure both compliance and effectiveness before the external auditor arrives! Also, it goes without saying that the internal audit process can be a far more enjoyable experience when everyone understands that the process is fundamentally designed to help everyone learn and improve.

Clause 9.3: Management Review

The management review meeting represents a forum where product and process objectives, measures, and goals are reviewed and assessed. It is a way to evaluate whether the quality management system is performing as projected, is economical, and is effective, and if any changes need to be introduced to increase quality or performance. These reviews must be conducted on a routine basis, even if the system is working to establish mitigation controls before any risks are actually encountered.

Reason

Value-added performance from your quality management system is a critical aspect of any good business practice. It is top managers who must "walk the talk" by reviewing ongoing performance and results of the company's products and services. Management support is mandatory to hold individuals accountable for customer satisfaction related to the jobs for which they are responsible. In a majority of instances, trained workers will continue to do their jobs and there may not be any outward appearance of a disconnect between their output and the quality expected by the customer. An internal audit, however, may reveal that work is not to the level of intended satisfaction because it has not met one or more requirements. Unfortunately, at that point, it may be too late for the company to recoup its reputation with the customer. This is where management reviews can help: They are conducted periodically to identify opportunities to improve. The management review process takes into consideration the inputs and outputs of all important processes and makes decisions that will identify problems and correct them before they occur.

Management reviews are critical for continual improvement. They act as a barometer to evaluate the health of the QMS and confirm that the QMS will continue to meet your business needs over time.

Implementation Guidance

Today's workforce is highly diversified and literally scattered around the globe. Based on where your stakeholders are located, you will have to make a decision regarding whether reviews are face to face, web based, or conducted via some other technology. Regardless of how the meetings are structured, management reviews are intended to improve the quality system, mitigate risks, and measure the QMS's impact. They are conducted with the same underlying intent as an audit—to evaluate the effectiveness of the QMS. The scope of the review should be comprehensive, although you need not review all the components of your QMS; that is, you should select the issues that have highest impact.

ISO 9001:2015 does not dictate the method you need to use for the management review. You can establish whatever method works best for your business. We have seen better results coming out of management reviews where specific results associated with QMS requirements are established up front, usually by taking into consideration the needs and experiences of cross-functional leaders. This allows for an easy comparison of pre-established goals and the results achieved. One useful approach has been to ask simple questions such as the following:

1. Have QMS-related goals been established for all cross-functional leaders?
2. What are the results we are getting from our QMS?
3. Are these results the ones we want relative to our pre-established goals?
4. Are we working on the right things?
5. Where do we need to implement change?
6. How do we make sure internally and externally changing circumstances are considered?
7. Which methodology will we use to track the recommendations from management reviews and the associated actions taken?

A management review can be considered successful when the discussion takes on an air of urgency, when attendees are eager to build their ideas atop others, and when the tempo and tone of the discussion feeds on its own energy. We've all seen the opposite scenario—the one where the quality manager simply presents a series of PowerPoint slides describing data that most everyone has seen before in one form or another. We suppose this approach can satisfy the definition of a "review," but it certainly does not rise to the level of an effective experience. Instead, use that same data to draw inferences and highlight trends, thereby opening the door to truly meaningful discussion.

A favorite phrase that can be applied during these meetings is "So what?" For example, if the topic at hand is the results of the audit, imagine asking the group some variation of "So what?" after presenting the raw data generated by past audits. All audits were on time, generated a dozen corrective actions, and were relatively well received. Asking "So what?" might generate a discussion about the significance of the program in general, such as whether audits are actually driving or truly helping management to make better decisions. Another management review topic is process performance and product conformance. Reams of paper and a plethora of PowerPoint slides have been devoted to explaining how the QMS is monitoring these areas, but the real question is whether things are conforming and effective and whether you have been properly monitoring the right things. In the face of any number of statistics regarding percentage of returns, throughput percentages, person-hours, and countless other data points, we encourage a management review that asks, "So what?"

Group discussions can provide a solid specific direction for the organization. The planning aspect is a significant first step to address if you want to obtain real benefits from the management review. Poorly planned reviews are a total waste of time and often result in frustration for management as well as the employees who are looking for direction from management. There is no specific requirement for the frequency of these meetings; that is an internal decision. You can conduct them as often as necessary, provided these meetings do not just become a venue for status reporting. To make them more meaningful and relevant, it is not uncommon for companies to conduct management reviews on a quarterly basis. This allows time for discussions to address new issues, make progress in regard to opportunities that were identified during previous reviews, and show small "wins," which are important for employee morale and customer satisfaction.

One question of importance to most companies is which elements must be considered during the management review. The answer is somewhat related to the five questions listed earlier. Recall that these reviews are intended to ensure all the performance targets are met to safeguard the robustness of your business. All of the work of planning and conducting management reviews will be for naught if you fail to consider the following critical elements:

- Actions taken from the previous management review, and the status and effectiveness of those actions.
- Analysis of the results of external or internal audits.
- Evaluation of the voice of the customer—for example, a review of customer data that correlates directly to customers' experiences, to evaluate what they are saying. The data can be collected from customer complaints, customer satisfaction surveys, one-on-one meetings, or user groups
- Status review of product performance and preexisting product-specific continuous improvement projects, problems encountered in products or services, associated risks, and the use of these reviews to mitigate the risks and address problems. For example:
  - Are problems related to the product or the process?
  - If they are product related, are they caused by hardware or software?

- Are they related to a supplier (evaluation of data and metrics focused on a supplier scorecard and the impacts of these results on business risks)?
- Is the impact business or legal?
- Are there any workarounds?

- Identification of areas where improvements can be made, development of the plan for improvement , and examination of human resources and their strategic deployment.
- Verification that there are sufficient resources available to address improvements. As potential changes are assessed, consider cross-functional plans and goals so that decisions can be integrated into your overall QMS.

In the end, we cannot emphasize enough that the conversation about continual improvement should not be relegated to just management reviews or an agenda item. It should be part of every employee's job to point out areas in need of improvement to benefit the company and its customers!

11

Clause 10: Improvement

At its core, ISO 9001 is designed to create an engine for improvement, a system that begins with carefully chosen objectives, calculated to meet or exceed customers' requirements in a competitive marketplace. Implementation of the various processes needed to achieve these objectives is carried out according to both the company's and ISO 9001's requirements, but invariably one or more problems result either within the company itself or once the final product or service is delivered. ISO 9001, however, is also designed to embrace the concept that problems are "opportunities in disguise" through application of the PDCA cycle. Clause 10 is not just the final segment of the ISO 9001:2015 standard; it is also the end of the PDCA cycle, the opportunity to *act* on problems that arose during the planned implementation of your QMS. Clause 10 is about improvement of that original plan; it helps the organization capitalize on the opportunity to reinvent or revise according to a set methodology for managing nonconformance. Most importantly, attention to Clause 10 impacts interested parties' perception of the company and its ability to professionally correct known process deficiencies.

Clause 10.1: General

Implementation

Improvement is progress. Thus far, the ISO 9001:2015 standard has offered a wealth of planning and implementation requirements that, taken as a whole, are reasoned, risk based, and objectively presented so as to create consistent, performing results. However, even the best planning may sometimes fall short, with severe consequences. It's interesting to note that instead of characterizing errors as a negative, the standard has chosen to call these lapses "opportunities for improvement." Indeed, they truly are. Learning from our mistakes and taking action to prevent further and future erosion of customer satisfaction—

even using a mistake or oversight to construct new and improved approaches to enhance satisfaction levels—can lead to an enormous positive response in the marketplace.

Naturally, it's always preferable to regularly monitor your important processes to ensure that results are as planned and receptive to any improvement possibilities. These include not only what it takes to improve customer satisfaction at the present moment, but also those improvements that are driven by future needs and possibilities within the marketplace. Nothing stands still forever, and as your products and services are tested it's inevitable that small corrections or even major breakthroughs will follow if the QMS is adequately tuned to the true needs and expectations of your customers. But when faced with those exceptions to proper planning—that is, when results are obviously below customer expectations—it's also imperative that the QMS be prepared to respond appropriately. Methodologies are discussed in clause 10.2.

Clause 10.2: Nonconformity and Corrective Action

Reason

Nonconformity is a planned result that does not meet expectations. Stories of perfect quality begin with "Once upon a time," for no better reason than that expressed by another well-worn adage: "The best-laid plans of mice and men often go astray." Clause 10.2 recognizes that a systematic approach to corrections and improvement is necessary to ensure that each side in a dispute can be heard and problems addressed using a logically developed approach with six working segments:

1. Define the problem completely and objectively.

2. Stop and correct the situation internally and/or externally.

3. If significant, analyze the consequences of the problem.

4. Determine the problem's most basic origin, its root cause.

5. Change the process that created the root cause.

6. Verify that the process change actually works.

These components are significant to your customers, as they build confidence in the ability of your QMS to self-correct. Moreover, when two companies are both registered to ISO 9001:2015, they naturally expect application of the identical approach when problems occur. Given that clause 10 requires your company to "implement necessary actions to meet customer requirements and enhance customer satisfaction," you should have confidence that your suppliers will also approach their mishaps in a similar manner. As you review the following discussion, think about how your organization might approach its supplier base to ensure those suppliers also use a process closely aligned to the organization's own to correct those situations that "go astray."

Implementation

Clause 10.2.1 presents a more detailed listing of actions to consider in the event of a "quality spill," or some similar negative event. For example, the problem could be a service center whose average wait time exceeds the planned minimum or the delivery of the right part at the wrong time. Each event is unique and often requires a unique response; however, as this clause mandates that documented information be maintained, most organizations begin the trail of documentation at this point. Clause 10.2.1a calls for the QMS to react to the issue "as applicable," precisely because of the range of possible problems that the average organization encounters in any given day. Is the problem internally or externally generated or discovered? What or who has been affected? Is the customer severely upset or simply calling to ask for a replacement? The opening section of the nonconformance record needs to be as clear and accurate as possible to assess its applicability to one or more expectations for the company's products or services.

What is important when making this assessment? After all, anyone in the organization may be the first person to learn of the nonconformity and the first individual to respond to the customer. Is a defined procedure readily available to offer guidance and possible referral to others whose job is to manage these situations? Is it clear among all those involved what constitutes an effective response? Here is where reference to clause 5.1 is appropriate, as top management's involvement and direction are prerequisites to guide these responses. If top managers passionately conveys their dedication to the QMS by appealing to and directing everyone to contribute to the effectiveness of the QMS, those employees who find themselves on the receiving end of a customer complaint can more confidently address the situation. To customers, the person to whom they are speaking is not just someone who works for the company; to them, that person *is* the company. Impressions are everything, and top management is the gatekeeper of these impressions and their consequences.

Clause 10.2 continues with the requirements to take action and manage the consequences of the nonconformity. Once again, it's important to record these activities. The correction may be as straightforward as a warranty return or direct replacement of a defective product, or as complex as a series of activities involving regulatory reporting and product recall. If the appropriate response is simple and will have negligible impact on either the company or the customer, the matter is recorded as "closed as correction," meaning that no further action is needed. In such a case, the problem has been solved with negligible impact and the odds of its reoccurrence are minimal. Of course, we are quick to reinforce the need for top management to define these parameters, for obvious reasons.

But when does a "correction" become a "corrective action"? That is, when is it appropriate to apply additional resources to dig into the nonconformity and its consequences to determine if further action is advisable? This is the essence of clause 10.2.1 b, and no doubt there will be many words written and statements made throughout the ISO community in an attempt to offer the perfect insight into what does and does not constitute proceeding from a correction to a corrective action. There is no silver bullet, no definitive prepackaged answer to offer in this regard, with the possible exception that all customer nonconformities become corrective actions if only because the infraction involved a customer whose impression of your company's quality may be instrumental to that organization's success. This approach is a variation of yet another adage: "The customer is always right." While that principle may seem questionable to some, it's often the Golden Rule to many whose QMS is built on the premise that customers, right or wrong, should be satisfied by either the initial transaction or the company's sincere reaction to problems arising from that transaction.

Regardless, clause 10.2.1b is a decision point. If it's clear that the QMS can't allow a repeat nonconformity, the path is set to apply additional time and energy to make sure that the problem won't happen again. This understanding is important because the commitment to proceed from this point onward is just that—a commitment to solve the problem to prevent its reoccurrence. When the company chooses corrective action, it decides to invest time and other resources to offset the costs of not doing so, and those costs can be considerable if testing and research are required to arrive at a proper root cause.

Clause 10.2.1b has three segments: analysis, determination of root cause, and further inquiry to determine if the problem may exist elsewhere in the system. The analysis of the situational description noted earlier is the starting point and the most easily accessible point of action. The corrective action may also require that additional interviews and data mining take place to frame an adequate understanding of the problem. Ultimately, these efforts are essential to developing the second and often most elusive component of corrective action: root cause.

Any number of books and articles have been written about root-cause analysis. We encourage you to become a student of "the five why's" or to learn how to use a "fishbone (Ishikawa) chart." Better still, and especially in the case of a large and important corrective action, you may want to investigate use of the "8-D approach." The method used for root-cause analysis is less important, however, than verifiable evidence that the nonconformity will not arise again in the future.

Verification is a test that affirms resources have been well spent and specifically that the discovered root cause was correct. Finding the proper root cause and not a further element of the nonconformity is often difficult for organizations. For each possible root cause, ask first if this is actually the true source of the nonconformity. For example, Jack may have been late for work, but the cause might be his broken alarm clock, and not because the drive to work took a few minutes more than expected. As another example, perhaps a machine created a series of out-of-spec parts not because of a momentary power failure, but because of a defective module in the machine.

Often, the corrective action is the opposite of the root cause. A process failure whose true root cause is the lack of a defined procedure can be corrected by writing the procedure and training all those involved; an injury caused by the lack of a machine guard can be corrected by the addition of the needed guard. After all, if the root cause indicates something lacking in the system, the addition of that component necessarily corrects the matter. The ISO 9001:2015 standard also requires that initial planning and considered risks be updated accordingly and that associated changes be made throughout the QMS, when needed. Identification of these risks may be difficult at first—most often the culprit may be a simple oversight. Of course, these oversights are also opportunities in waiting because the organization is learning and improving, especially as it considers the next round of analysis of its interested parties and the risks attached to doing business.

As an example, consider the call center whose initial understanding of the potential demand for customer inquiries was guided by an inaccurate assessment of the impact of a new design to its flagship product. Instead of the expected volume of calls, the actual number of customer inquiries was twice the expected number. A corrective action was instigated when complaints rose to an unprecedented level. The root cause was determined using the "five why's" method: The new design caused customers to question whether their existing system was capable of incorporating other, unseen changes without an upgrade, even though this was clearly indicated in the product literature. Two corrective actions resulted: (1) Future designs will now carry more clearly articulated product interoperability notices and (2) the number of call center operators will be doubled for a three-month period after the initial launch of new designs.

Finally, and as mentioned previously, a nonconformity can take any size or shape, affect one or a hundred, collapse a component or the entire organization. Therefore, care must be applied when determining the organization's response to nonconformance. Just as the law seeks to make the punishment fit the crime, so too should the response to nonconformance be measured in direct proportion to its actual impact, both now and in the future. Many organizations are proactive, establishing separate committees to review nonconformances and determine an effective path forward. Making these decisions with a top manager as an active team member is an added plus, as it provides evidence of the manager's commitment to the success and effectiveness of the QMS.

Clause 10.3: Continual Improvement

Reason

Improvement is not just progress, but growth. A QMS that is using all its inputs (e.g., corrective actions, risk-based thinking, internal audits, management reviews) and listening closely to its customers' reactions to its products is an engine of improvement that is almost constantly growing the appreciation of its processes and systems. Growth is therefore not only financial in nature, though there is certainly much to be said for profitability and reward. Profits are, however, the result of other forms of growth that precede the financial results—growth in not only product acceptance but also your organization's abilities to consistently provide conforming product in the face of increasing (and justified!) demand.

Implementation

Clause 10.3 is less a set of requirements and more a call to recognize those elements of the QMS that currently are improving or can improve in the future. Any number of metrics will have been established along the way in the development of your QMS, each of which you should be routinely monitoring and applying additional resources when needed. Determining the suitability of these actions is often as easy as analyzing next month's metrics or conducting a special audit of the process in question. Management review, analysis and evaluation efforts, internal audits, and indeed all of clause 9 requirements are fundamental to the depth of improvement you can expect as an outcome. Establishment of a QMS according to the requirements of ISO 9001:2015 is an improvement effort in itself—the one we have tried to help you achieve throughout this book. An effective QMS is synonymous with improvement, because it's designed for that purpose. In fact, ISO 9001:2015's chief benefit is that collectively, each requirement is built atop others whose cumulative effect is to manage the ultimate risk of not instituting ISO 9001 in the first place. The standard, in essence, provides guidance to improve.

We hope we've been helpful in guiding your efforts. We trust that once your QMS is fully operational, improvement will no longer be a goal but a given within your company.

12

Restating the Value Added and Enablement Perspective

Over their more than 25 years as quality experts with hands-on experience, the authors of this book have seen the value of implementing quality management systems. ISO 9001 provides a good set of foundational elements for you to start your own journey toward addressing quality concerns and improving customer satisfaction. But beware: If your organization is one of those companies that is implementing ISO 9001 for the sake of getting a framed certificate so it can get additional sales, then you will not achieve necessary results. In contrast, if you take quality seriously and make a decision to pursue "best-in-class" concepts, implementing the standard will be your first step. In this chapter, we discuss other excellence methodologies that can take you beyond ISO 9001, if you so desire.

Throughout this book, you have seen that the ISO 9001:2015 standard emphasizes areas of your business that need attention for enhancing customers' experiences. In this section, we once again summarize the value added by following a methodology that has been adopted by millions of users worldwide.

- **Satisfaction of customer requirements.** Many companies' customers are requiring ISO certification before they will do business with a vendor. Customers realize that vendors' poor quality will affect them negatively. They also know that through the basic exercise of obtaining ISO 9001 certification, a company will have to put certain processes in place, train its employees in quality management system principles, and ensure its adherence to processes, thereby raising quality awareness within the organization.

- **Improved quality of products and services.** It is becoming crystal clear that companies must follow a systematic approach to improve the quality of their products and services, which in turn may result in greater efficiency and market share. For many, it will become cost prohibitive to design their own structured approach, as doing so requires additional human resources, understanding of what needs to be done, and company-wide buy-in. ISO 9001 is a known quality management system, and one of the positive outcomes of its effective implementation can be seen in regard to the quality of the company's products and services.

- **Increased productivity.** Having a company-wide, consistent quality management system eliminates the need for individuals to create their own mini-systems, thereby saving hundreds of experimental hours. The communication between functional departments will become easier once everyone understands the common language. In turn, intergroup coordination will become smoother, eliminating the need for extra communications and meetings, and allowing more time for innovation.

- **Improved customer satisfaction.** Hello! If this is not the strongest driver, then what else is? A well-defined, well-understood implementation of ISO 9001 requires discipline to follow pre-established processes and tenacity to really understand customer requirements. Time and again, it has been proven that the end results of these two components together are better quality and improved customer satisfaction.

- **Higher employee morale.** When employees know that their company emphasizes customer satisfaction and quality, that realization boosts the employees' morale. Employees who are happy tend to work harder, are motivated, and stay loyal to the company, resulting is less turnover (and turnover is a high expense). You should start worrying if your company has high employee turnover, because on average it takes a new employee approximately 90 days to learn the job and fit into the new culture. Keeping employee morale high is one of the best ways you can foster a productive workplace.

- **Focus on continual improvement.** The internal audits associated with ISO 9001 are leading indicators of nonconformance. They serve as a tool with which to improve problematic areas and to identify best practices. To promote quality, the requirements outlined in ISO 9001 can be shared with other functional departments within your company, thus enabling good practices.

- **Control over your business.** One of the requirements of ISO 9001 is metrics that help you understand what is working and what is not working in the performance of your system, permitting you to implement necessary changes in those elements that are not working and to eliminate waste. By examining trends in these metrics, you will be able to understand your business better and be in a position to develop initiatives for further improvements.

When they understand the execution and observance of requirements outlined in the ISO 9001 quality management standards, both employees and managers will be in a position to emphasize and focus on what is advantageous for the business and what will give it a competitive edge.

Managing the Quality System

By its very nature, the quality system is a complex system. In large companies, it may be as dense and convoluted as practicing medicine or piloting a modern commercial jetliner. And though it may appear that those who excel in these disciplines are universally bright and insightful, the best will be quick to tell you that the only thing that really matters is results. The best and brightest may be far more capable of understanding complexities and arguing one or more theories to support their positions, but without a clear vision of what those theories are designed to accomplish, results will be slow in coming and harder still to maintain. Results are also inevitable, since planned or unplanned outcomes typically become public, gain special momentum if negative, and have the power to rebut even the most vocal critics if positive. Results are also what top management needs to validate their various investments in operations and quality. Everyone knows that "we're working on it" is not a result, and that at its best this response has a limited lifespan. Having a plan with clearly defined deliverables enables results, and even though each milestone may be little more than a progress check, it is still the result of a predefined plan.

Ultimately, managing a QMS or any management program is about results that are measured against a plan. Complexities live and thrive within the many overlapping and intersecting plans that abound in all companies. Management's awareness and understanding of schedules and targets is important, but it is equally important that all of these programs and projects are functioning well in relation to one another. This need for coordination poses a challenge when companies are developing new or managing existing quality systems. While a QMS is by its very nature a complexity, it need not be overly complicated to develop a meaningful report on its progress. Clarity is the goal of all reporting, and the clearest approach to sharing information on the failures and successes of the QMS is already contained in clause 9—specifically, clause 9.3, "Management Review." The separate subclauses under clause 9.3 provide a well-structured set of discussion topics, each related to activities that should be driving improvement within the organization.

Management review has traditionally been a compliance-based activity—that is, something that must be done for the sake of maintaining ISO 9001 registration. It need not be this way, of course. The status of many separate goals and functions of your QMS is already obvious to most managers on a daily or weekly basis. They already know that customers are either upset or praising your products. They may already know there is a major problem in production or that development of a particular design is lagging woefully behind its second promised launch date. What they may *not* know is how many of these individual problems or successes are contributing to each other—that is, which interconnections are functioning within the QMS to either enable or disable progress toward the goal. Excellent management reviews are a catalyst for discussions about these problems and enable managers to concentrate on significant underlying issues if the organizer carefully analyzes and presents possible trends within or shared by one or more processes. For example, a company's manufacturing problems might be creating customer satisfaction issues while management is concerned about the price of raw materials and has been highly vocal in its call to find alternative suppliers. There is an obvious cause and effect in play in this scenario, and "process performance and conformity of products and services" (clause 9.3.1.3c) is obviously relevant as the best place to start the conversation. But why wait for a "planned interval" to start the conversation? Why is it that management reviews are held only annually or semiannually, when issues such as these do not adhere to any set schedule?

The obvious answer is to define the "planned intervals" for management reviews in whatever span you choose, but to note that special meetings are determined by QMS results. This way, one or more influences can drive the call for a special meeting to discuss targeted specifics. As the review manager, your job is to select the most appropriate 9.3 subclause as the framework for discussion, present suitable charts and graphs, or simply outline the interrelations that appear to be influencing one or more objectives. In other words, sessions that address management review issues can be spread out throughout the year and jump from one subclause to another in the process. The requirement to retain documented information (records), of course, continues to be part of this "distributed approach."

Managing a QMS is also best distributed among the management team, per clause 5.3, "Organizational Roles, Responsibilities, and Authorities." The past method of assigning a single person who becomes responsible for the quality program should be abandoned in favor of distributing these responsibilities among a group. This approach represents a major advance in combining quality and business, wherein the management group works as a team in developing and monitoring the program.

As you manage the QMS, be aware that some employees are likely to resist its application; there will be always be a few who are against definition and accountability, especially the latter. Those whose work carried little or no oversight in the past typically resist efforts to monitor their progress or calls to work in accordance with new procedures and goals. Change is not easy, especially for this group, and the 2015 revision of ISO 9001 is a call for many changes. As revised or new clauses in the standard become elements that are managed, resistance will inevitably appear. But if the management team prepares carefully and presents its case for moving forward in one voice with ISO 9001:2015, a large majority of employees can be expected to follow their lead. The keys to success are twofold: (1) distributing the responsibilities for managing the QMS and (2) presenting the revised approach as a team effort by management.

Results should be managed as a team effort, with relevant personnel meeting regularly, but called together when special issues become apparent. This is the best prescription for successful management of your QMS and replaces the concept that quality is the province of a single person or department.

Further Improvement Opportunities for Implementers: Business Excellence Methodologies

When we talk about improvement opportunities, we are referring to use of a systematic approach, using a specific method, with structured activities to improve quality, thereby achieving success with customer satisfaction, desired customer experience, and sustainable results. Excellence methodologies constitute a set of activities that are carried out to address different elements of quality; they are intended to drive a cultural shift, a change in how you evolve from where you are. Fixing internal pain-points to drive productivity, growth, and customer experience is a quest that is more internally oriented within your company, and you have to be the advocate for improvement activities and focus on business issues that affect these efforts. Fixing singular functional issues will deliver results only slowly, however. What you really need is an overall framework that can address company-wide challenges, thereby eliminating problematic issues that hinder adoption of your products or services. Put simply, business excellence methodologies or frameworks are needed as customer behaviors and needs change.

A wide variety of quality management and quality improvement methodologies are available, and the selection of which is right for your organization requires development of an in-depth strategy based on the outcomes that you would like to achieve. Before you start, the organization's goals must be established and plans must be developed to achieve those goals. Today, despite many reasons for implementing business excellence methodologies, a surprisingly cohesive set of principles arises among these tools:

- A "voice of the customer first" orientation
- Reduction of product/service variations
- Emphasis on early prevention, than correction
- Standardization, which saves money and resources

- Emphasis on the design phase of the product or service, thereby doing it right the first time
- Involvement of all internal stakeholders
- Focus on increasing market share and customer base
- Gaining customer confidence by delivering defect-free products and services

Once you have decided to spend energy and resources on improving the customer experience, it becomes obvious that just one corporate quality department will not be able to address this broad subject and the understanding of what needs to be done. Instead, this concern spans the entire organization and touches every job. All constituents of the company must be involved both initially and as the program or framework evolves. Failure to plan the quality framework properly will contribute to a loss of momentum and employee confidence in the program.

The most critical component is obtaining management commitment, so that even in times of great pressure, the quality and "customer comes first" attitude is preserved. Changing organization culture is equally important, as employees usually become accustomed to doing things in a certain way and find it difficult to change their behavior. Unless you have provided solid reasons why the behavior must change, do not expect anyone to follow and change for you! The question "What's in it for me?" must be answered. Investing extra time in two-way communication between management and employees is certainly worth the effort. Speeches, campaigns, off-site meetings, and similar techniques will have only short-term effects. By comparison, spending more time up front in planning, implementing, and training for the business excellence framework will provide for a greater chance of success.

Instead of implementing the full framework on a company-wide basis from day 1, our suggestion is to run a trial program first. All individuals who will be involved in the program should be trained eventually, but initially training can be provider for just those who will be involved in the trial program and key members of each functional area. Once the trial program has produced a few successes, you can then take it company-wide.

In the next sections, we examine some of the more popular process evaluation frameworks. There is no consensus as to which framework or method will guarantee the best results; thus it is in your best interest to objectively evaluate each and select the one that best meets your requirements, and to provide a well-thought-out plan for its deployment in your organization.

Six Sigma

Today's competitive environment leaves no room for even the slightest margin of error. To delight your customers, you have to not just meet their expectations, but strive to exceed those expectations. The main idea behind Six Sigma is to put a process in place that ensures that you systematically reduce the defects to no more than 3.4 defects per 1 million opportunities. Within this framework, opportunities are defined in terms of meeting customer requirements. Six Sigma is a rigorous process for anticipating and solving problems, which is intended to yield improved revenues and profits through defect reduction and improved customer satisfaction. The basic concepts for this framework come from a program initiated by Motorola in the 1980s.

The term "sigma" signifies how a product or service is meeting the requirements of the customers. The goal of 3.4 defects per 1 million opportunities means failing to meet a customer requirement only 3.4 times out of 1 million opportunities. Transitioning from 3-sigma to 6-sigma results in nearly a 20,000-fold reduction in defects.

Six Sigma principles and practices help companies to:

- **Improve productivity.** When businesses use the Six Sigma methodology, they allocate experienced employees within the organization to identify areas that would negatively affect the targeted project and the outcome. These individuals are chartered to identify solutions for these areas, and the process facilitates shorter cycle times for projects by identifying and resolving problematic areas right from the beginning.

- **Win customer care war and loyalty.** Customer loyalty is associated with a very high degree of customer satisfaction, and winning the customer care war requires a high caliber of employees. These employees are trained to listen to customers and address customer concerns in a relatively short time, while simultaneously managing customer expectations by delivering solutions for problems that require in-depth analysis.

  You will be able to manage customer expectations if the customer is well informed of the steps that are being taken and there is frequent communication. Following a structured Six Sigma approach helps the organization better understand customer requirements and be able to build, deliver, and support products and services that meet or exceed customer satisfaction expectations and reduce the risk of unsatisfied customers.

- **Drive revenue growth.** While revenue growth might seem like a straightforward process dependent on increased advertising and hiring a seasoned salesforce, it is quite a daunting task. A number of factors may affect revenue:

  - Demand for the product or service
  - Cost
  - Ease of purchasing
  - Ease of use

  - Products and services offered by competitors

  And the list goes on.

One given is that revenue growth is associated with the quality of the product or service and trained customer support from the company. Six Sigma promotes quality and training, resulting in ongoing growth, and creates blissful customer service experiences. As a consequence, revenue growth and new levels of corporate profitability are achieved.

- **Increase employee satisfaction.** Six Sigma concepts start with top managers, who need to be fully engaged. Companies where management supports quality efforts, walks the talk, recognizes employees for high performance, and holds individuals accountable for results have seen an increase in productivity and employee loyalty. Employee satisfaction translates into a happy workforce, whose members respect and care for customers and become more productive. In addition, satisfied employees doing quality work can help the company gain more customers and a larger market share.

    The Six Sigma problem-solving tools and techniques support employee development and help create a climate for employee motivation.

- **Improve the supply chain.** Supply chain management has a direct impact on products or services and the overall profitability of the company. Thus, to improve profitability, Six Sigma places greater emphasis on the quality of the supply chain. Improving the supply chain's efficiency by inspecting suppliers' processes and focusing on efforts to implement quality control within the supply chain can prevent wastage of materials and loss of time.

- **Achieve continual improvement.** The Six Sigma framework helps organizations focus on areas where there are significant opportunities for improvement.

The Six Sigma Process

The Six Sigma framework has simple steps, but requires organizational vigor and discipline to yield the desired results. It is built around five concepts: define, measure, analyze, improve, and control (DMAIC; Figure 12.1). Each of these concepts is associated with tools and techniques that can guide you through the process from beginning to end.

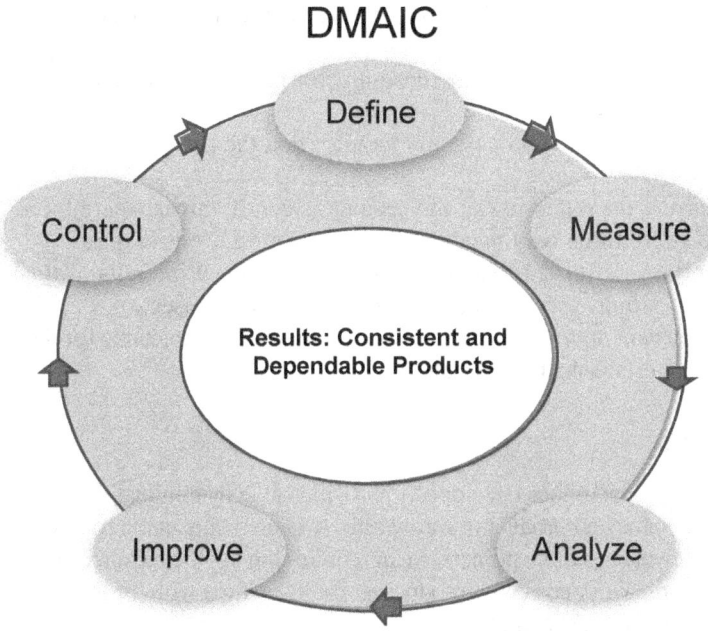

Figure 12.1 *DMAIC: Define, Measure, Analyze, Improve, and Control*

- **Define** the customers and what their requirements are for products and services, define the project and opportunities for improvement, and define the process to be improved.
- **Measure** the performance of the process, collect data to determine the problems and metrics, and determine the gaps.
- **Analyze** the data to identify the root causes of the problems and determine the opportunities for improvement.
- **Improve** the process by redesigning to prevent the root causes, develop an improvement plan, and deploy the new process.
- **Control** the improvements to ensure the process continues according to the goals and does not deviate from the plan.

The main elements of Six Sigma center on understanding your customers, knowing your suppliers, knowing your process, and knowing whether the process is working. As further guidance, here is a list of pertinent considerations to begin with:

- Know who your customers are, what they are saying about your products and services, and what their requirements are.
- Define what your product or service is for the customer.
- Select the suppliers that you will need.

- Identify the process you have to follow to develop the product or offer the service.
- Incorporate the customer needs into the design before the development of the product or service begins.
- Train the staff to carry out the process and monitor that the process is being followed.
- Periodically measure the outcomes of the products; identify areas where there are problems and determine why the defects are occurring. Control these defects effectively by defining robust processes, thereby ensuring reliability and consistency so as to improve what the customer receives and uses.
- Evaluate where you can improve further, and hold individuals accountable for their adherence to the pre-established processes.

Lean Six Sigma

Lean is a technique and set of activities developed to provide value by eliminating activities that do not add value and producing zero waste. A Lean organization focuses on key processes to increase value to its customers. Lean requires having the resources with the right expertise, doing the work correctly, producing results on time with the desired quality, and making sure there is no wastage.

Given that the Lean technique focuses on eliminating waste and the Six Sigma tools focus on improving quality, both of these approaches are often employed simultaneously, with the desired result being improved efficiency. Indeed, most companies now implement Lean Six Sigma rather than just the Six Sigma framework by itself.

Total Quality Management

Total quality management (TQM) is a discipline that has been a key to success for many organizations. Its application crosses several industries, and TQM has been implemented globally by numerous organizations. For TQM to succeed, four "pillars" must be addressed:

- Customer focus
- Leadership mindset and commitment
- Employee empowerment
- Total involvement of process improvement

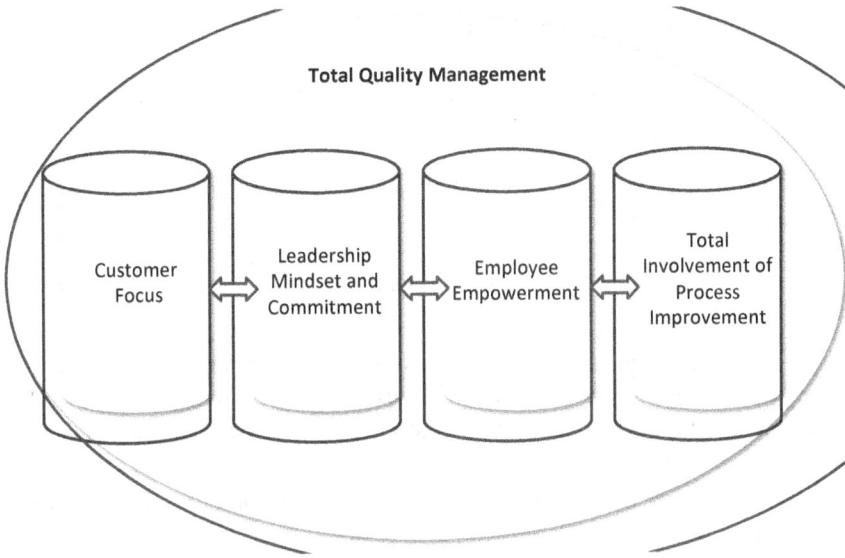

Figure 12.2 *Pillars of TQM*

Customer Focus

The adage that "The customer is king" has to be taken seriously—everything begins and ends with the customer! The decision to initially purchase the product or service is made by the customer, the act of using it falls to the customer, the phone calls for questions or complaints are made by the customer, the decision to continue doing the business with the selling organization is made by the customer, the decision to repurchase is made by the customer, and so on. What this really means is clear for the organization: If a customer is not happy with how his requirements are met, the decision to stop doing business will be made without any hesitation, and the bottom line for the company will be negatively affected if this trend continues among other customers.

Everything that the company does should revolve around the customer. A high-quality customer experience starts with the initial contact but continues through after-sales care. In this sense, it does not matter if the customer returns for subsequent purchases or is just a one-time buyer: It is the ease of doing business and the quality of the company's product or service that matters! A number of factors may affect customers' experiences throughout their buying journey:

- Initial purchase:
  - How easy is it to understand the marketing literature?
  - Is someone available to assist the customer by addressing questions and concerns?
  - Is the company receptive to customer needs and wants?

- If licensing or warranty is involved, is each of these items explained properly?
- How long did it take to get the purchase delivered to the customer?

- Implementation and use:
  - How easy is it to implement and use the product or service?
  - How reliable is the product or services
  - How often is there a breakdown?
  - What is the mean time between each breakdown?

- Customer support:
  - How easy is to reach someone at the customer support desk?
  - How often is the support person able to resolve the problem?
  - How much time does it take for the customer-support person to get back to the customer with resolution of the problem?
  - If a warranty is involved, how difficult is it for the customer to make claims under the warranty?

- Complaint procedure:
  - How cumbersome is it to file a complaint?
  - Is the customer consistently informed of the status of the complaint?
  - How long does it take to resolve a complaint?
  - How much time does it take to get back to the customer?

Leadership Mindset and Commitment

It is the leaders of the company who encourage employees to be customer-centric and who act as role models. Almost anyone who is in a leadership position can command commitment, but it is the leader who inspires commitment by exhibiting values who encourages employees to be dedicated and work harder to be top producers. Leaders have to be the spokespersons for their organization's goals and the strategies, conveying the message of why it is important for every individual to get involved in the mission of pursuing continuous improvement.

The first demonstration of leadership commitment is the allocation of appropriate resources and funding for ongoing training so that appropriate staff can stay on top of the technology and the industry best practices. At the same time, training on TQM itself is very critical for the employees so that the entire employee base will understand its concepts. We have seen cases where the senior leaders did not attend the TQM training, but rather delegated middle managers to be in charge of the training and ensure that everyone else attends. When top managers do not get the same training, this sends the completely wrong message and indicates that those leaders are not really interested in the TQM program.

It is the top leaders who must hold individuals accountable when pre-established processes are not used, by stressing that adherence is just as important as achieving the results and continuously excelling. We understand the need for deviations to the pre-established practices, based on the urgency of specific situations. However, such deviations should be few and far between, with authorized individuals signing off on them only after ensuring the risks have been evaluated and mitigation already considered.

For the TQM framework to work and be sustained over time, everyone must understand the overall company direction. Leaders must take time from their busy schedules to engage with employees and convey the message, and they must be consistent regarding the intent of the program. Frequent communications through employee meetings, individual focus groups, and email are encouraged. Open, two-way communication channels must be highlighted so that employees feel comfortable in approaching the leadership with their concerns.

Continuous improvement is a journey based on capturing ongoing metrics of the organization's progress toward its goals. It is the company's managers who, based on the metrics, decide whether a change of direction is needed. Strong leaders are aware of where the company is going, whether the quality management system is working, and when it should be tweaked to get better results.

Implementing and executing an employee reward system, fostering job security, and creating a collaborative culture reflect leaders' sincere commitment to TQM.

Employee Empowerment

Based on our research, it appears that most employees place a very high importance on getting public recognition: They like it when their leaders make public announcements about the importance of their contributions. They believe that this type of recognition empowers them to continue to perform at their best. When staff feel they are empowered to make decisions and are respected for taking risks, they care about their leaders and demonstrate their high satisfaction by becoming active supporters of the leaders.

Highly satisfied employees will make sure their leaders do not fail, owing to the mutual respect and trust created by the leader–follower relationship. They will make a greater commitment to the company and the work assigned. Involving employees and including them in the decision process also provides an opportunity for the organization to get more innovative ideas to develop better products and services, identify problems, and come up with new ways to save money. Such suggestions may mean the difference between success and failure for the organization.

Total Involvement of Process Improvement

Functional organizations are dependent upon one another. For example, sales personnel must be supported by the marketing staff and the customer support department, if they are to succeed. If one department follows the principles of TQM and another does not, however, the positive end results will not be as dramatic as if both had implemented TQM. The interdependency between organizations dictates total involvement of every department and every employee in the improvement efforts. Company-wide attention to what is not working and what needs to be corrected, awareness of customer pain-points, and the rewards of doing the right thing must be understood. For this reason, as noted earlier, everyone in the organization must participate in the TQM training, including the leadership.

Human beings are creatures of habit. When was the last time you decided to change the route when going from your home to your regular grocery store for weekly shopping? If there are no other errands to be conducted, we generally take the same route because we know how long it will take to go there, we are familiar with the surroundings, and we do not have to incur the stress of finding a new way. Similarly, even if some of the processes throughout the company are newly established but the affected employees are not required to adopt and adhere to them, there will be some who will adopt the new processes and others who will continue to do same old thing.

Every employee and every functional team must become part of the TQM movement and make a pledge—a commitment—to customer success. In addition to what you do, how you do it will have a profound impact on the ultimate results achieved by your organization.

In summary, the plan to implement the TQM program starts with the top leadership, who must provide support by removing obstacles and creating an environment for everyone to succeed.

ISO 9004

ISO 9004 is the least appreciated quality management standard. To date, we have not seen many companies where its concepts have been implemented. The same committee that develops and maintains ISO 9001:2015, TC176/SC2, handles these responsibilities for ISO 9004. The current version of this standard is ISO 9004:2009, "Managing for the Sustained Success of an Organization: A Quality Management Approach." This least celebrated quality management approach is not used for certifying your organization, but rather is intended for internal use and complements the requirements of ISO 9001. If implemented and used to the full extent, it assists in achieving sustained success and improving performance and is intended to go beyond the requirements of ISO 9001. The ISO 9004 standard can be used along with ISO 9001:2015 to achieve long-term results. Such sustained success enables a company to stake out a strong and advantageous competitive position. If that position is maintained on an ongoing basis, the organization can achieve strong financial performance quarter after quarter, its stock will retain a high value, and both its shareholders and Wall Street in general will be happy with its growth.

The ISO 9004 standard has set of guidelines or recommendations, which are not mandatory. These principles or suggestions, if implemented correctly, can definitely benefit your organization. Before the release of ISO 9001:2015, ISO 9004 mirrored the clauses of ISO 9001, with potential improvements associated with each guideline.

The highlight of ISO 9004 is its self-assessment tool. With this tool, users determine the maturity levels of different elements and, therefore, the state of their organization, by identifying strengths and weaknesses as well as improvement opportunities. The self-assessment tool covers the following areas:

- Management and leadership
- Strategy and policy
- Process management
- Resource management
- Monitoring and measurement
- Improvement, innovation, and learning

Note that ISO 9004 promotes the concept of process assessment, which other ISO standards address via a similar approach. These standards cover different aspects of organizational maturity, depending on the industry. For example, the ISO 15504 series provides guidance on concepts of process assessments and performing them. ISO 33004 covers the relationship between maturity models and process assessment models. ISO 21827 covers the Systems Security Engineering Capability Maturity Model, while ISO 16680 highlights the Open Group Service Integration Maturity Model.

The Software Engineering Institute at Carnegie Mellon developed the Capability Maturity Model—Integrated (CMMI), which is a structured and systematic set of best practices for process improvement. During CMMI assessment, maturity level ratings are determined based on the evaluations of implementation and results of specific practices outlined in the CMMI framework.

All of these standards, guidelines, and assessment tools provide good information, and their application will enable your organization to go beyond the basic quality fundamentals of ISO 9001.

Malcolm Baldrige Award

Established by the U.S. Congress in 1987, the Malcolm Baldrige Award is given to U.S. companies that have successfully implemented quality management systems. The award's name honors Malcom Baldrige, who was Secretary of Commerce from 1981 until his death in a rodeo accident in July 1987. Baldrige was a promoter of quality management and took great interest in the quality improvement act, which was later named after him. The purpose of the Malcolm Baldrige Award is to raise awareness of quality management.

Awards may be given to companies in six different categories: service, manufacturing, small business, health care, education, and nonprofit. Seven criteria are evaluated in relation to the award:

- Leadership
- Strategic planning
- Customer and market focus
- Measurement, analysis, and knowledge management
- Human resources focus
- Process management
- Business/organization performance results

Organizations that are headquartered in the United States can apply for the award. Their applications are evaluated by quality experts from the industry; these independent examiners review each application for results and improvements in all of the seven previously mentioned categories. The organizations that pass the initial screening are visited by the examiners, who meet with various individuals to inspect and verify the accuracy of the data supplied in the application. At the end of the verification activity, the organization receives a written report on each criterion, noting its strengths and areas for improvement. The applicants that excel in all the criteria may receive the award, which is given by the president of United States. Since the purpose of the award is to promote quality management, the winners are required to share their best practices with other organizations.

We have listed some of the common business excellence methodologies here, but there are many others. Many countries have their own excellence models, similar to the U.S. Malcolm Baldrige award.

ISO 9001 as a Foundation and Enabler

Those practitioners who have openly wondered, "How do we get to the next level?" ask this question for a reason. Perhaps quality output is a concern, employees are leaving, sales are flat, or a new program has once again proven to deliver just "more of the same." Most organizations are acutely aware of their context and the successes of others in the same field. Simple growth aside, it sometimes seems as if other organizations have found a secret to success, some unknown system that helped them move forward to that always-elusive "next level." Perhaps impassioned founders create new products, momentum, and purpose; a great idea becomes the next "monster app"; or the unexpected acceptance of new features or customer interaction sends the stock price soaring and ushers in an era of new growth and expansion. While these scenarios have certainly occurred, most organizations can only look on with admiration and a degree of wonder, still asking themselves what might be done to move forward in a more focused and successful manner. But stop and ask which attributes these companies have in common, and the following points will likely become evident:

- They work as a team.
- They know what must be done.

- They constructed working processes to enable communication and teamwork.
- They carefully monitor progress toward known goals.
- Their leaders are passionately involved.
- They actively listen to their customers.
- They remain flexible.
- They expect success.

ISO 9001:2015 can be implemented to achieve all of these attributes and enable your organization to realize its vision. Starting with clause 4 and the requirements to plan based on context and to determine the wants and needs of interested parties, the standard goes on to present a roadmap for achieving your company's chosen objectives. The 2015 revision is the closest the ISO 9001 standard has come to blurring the lines between quality and business, and it has done so deliberately. Your application of the standard determines what can be accomplished. And as those plans mature, use of the standard can enable you to monitor progress toward those goals your organization has identified.

ISO 9001:2015 is foundational to best practices. Great companies, whether registered to ISO 9001 or not, share the very same approach as they set their employees to work within carefully planned groups to accomplish important things — things they believe to be necessary to meet one or more business goals. Their aim was not to certify because their customers demanded it, but rather to achieve a higher level of business excellence and market share.

Your application of ISO 9001:2015 as an enabler of excellence has been a central theme throughout this book; one that will require recognizing the standard's new format and requirements not as an imposition, but as the helpmeets they were intended. The 2015 revision is a roadmap to that next level you may be searching for, because it was designed by experts to enable companies to achieve their goals. ISO 9001:2015 enables each organization to apply its resources to what it wants to become.

A

The Quality Management Principles

The 2000 revision of ISO 9001 was an important change from the past, in which an entirely new structure and additional clauses presented much the same challenges as the current 2015 revision. The 2000 revision was disruptive, requiring companies to change clause structure or provide equivalency matrices. The new requirements, which were foundational to the process approach, customer focus, and additional management responsibilities, were in many ways without deep footings to help organizations find value in and reasoning for these changes. The original eight quality management principles (QMPs) were developed to create these footings, but the advent of the high-level structure and the resulting changes within ISO 9001:2015 generated new interest in the possibility of revising the QMPs in light of these changes. The result is the current seven QMPs that, while close to their predecessors, are in many respects easier to use and understand. Both ISO 9001:2015 and ISO 9000:2015 devote some discussion to these principles (more so than ISO 9000), in that key benefits and actions for improvement of each principle are described.

The seven quality management principles are as follows:

QMP 1: Customer focus
QMP 2: Leadership
QMP 3: Engagement of people
QMP 4: Process approach
QMP 5: Improvement
QMP 6: Evidence-based decision making
QMP 7: Relationship management

Instead of copying and expanding on several online sources (perhaps the best of which is a brochure developed by ISO Central Secretariat [ISBN 978-92-67-10650-2]), we will approach these principles in a more holistic manner by examining the sequence and overall connectedness of these seven powerful concepts.

It all begins with an appreciation of the customer. Without the customer's acceptance of your product, there is no business. It is a simple fact—some would say "Business 101"—that a clear focus on the customer's wants and needs is the essence of developing and maintaining positive communication that will continually pay benefits to both sides of any contract.

But once those wants and needs are understood, how can an organization succeed in supplying goods and services that will satisfy its clients? What should be the next step that the company should address that satisfies its clients? The answer is, getting the right leadership. The first responsibility of leadership is to clearly describe the customer's position to those who will supply the product or service. Leaders not only focus on the customer, but often build the facility to create what the customers want. Eventually, they are also central to bringing the voice of the customer to those employees who work for them.

Those workers are vitally important to the entire process, as their engagement—their contribution to making what the customer wants—is foundational to maintaining the supply of the goods and services. These employees are important to understand customer needs. In many organizations, they are internal customers whose contributions are instrumental in determining quality, velocity, cost, and countless other components of managing and producing.

But how can these people maximize their output? More broadly, how can organizations as a whole continue to evolve and grow? What is foundational to moving from concept to reality, and subsequently maintaining gains while also actively improving quality and satisfaction? The use of the process approach, which entails first moving through the Deming cycle of plan, do, check, act (PDCA) and then managing both processes and the system of processes as an improvement engine, creates a momentum for maximizing excellence and growth.

The company that succeeds in maintaining a customer focus, provides leadership, engages its people, and uses the process approach is one that is continually improving. The regular analysis of key performance indicators provides new sources of action to improve results. The overall design for providing what the customer wants keeps the company growing in its efficiencies and becoming more effective by design. This kind of organization is succeeding.

In such a company, decisions are not based on hunches or speculation, but rather on facts. Market research, higher levels of sales involvement, and numerous internal reporting tools are routinely routed to everyone in the company. In the process, data and information become the currency of continued success. The acquisition of new equipment is driven by maintenance records and analysis of a machine's life cycle, just as the decision to expand the sales offices is the result of traffic studies. The era of the "wish list" has given way to fact/evidence-based decision making.

None of these principles, however, can be truly effective without understanding that companies and individuals must work together to their mutual benefit. You are the customer of your supplier, just as you are the supplier to your customer. This relationship is summarized by the Golden Rule: "Do unto others as you would have them do unto you." It is a win-win proposition that encourages growth if only because mutual respect and trust usher in honesty and willingness to work together to conduct business.

And now we have come full circle! As each company within this chain of suppliers and customers follows the seven management principles, the collective effort toward always improving becomes beneficial to all.

B

Other Standards

In this book we have offered implementation advice and explained each clause of ISO 9001:2015. However, there are other standards that are used by many organizations worldwide. Here, we have cited many of those that can help you in further improving your quality management system, along with some sector-specific and other helpful documents. These resources will be supportive as you go through the journey of increasing your knowledge base of relevant industry standards. Note that this is not a complete list. We suggest that you research one or more standards in your area of interest if one does not appear on this list.

Standard	Year Published
ISO 9000 Quality Management Systems: Fundamentals and Vocabulary	**2015**
ISO 9004 Managing for the Sustained Success of an Organization: A Quality Management Approach	**2004**
ISO 10001 Quality Management: Customer Satisfaction: Guidelines for Codes of Conduct for Organizations	**2007**
ISO 10002 Quality Management: Customer Satisfaction: Guidelines for Complaints Handling in Organizations	**2014**
ISO 10003 Quality Management: Customer Satisfaction: Guidelines for Dispute Resolution External to Organizations	**2007**

Standard	Year Published
ISO 10004 Quality Management: Customer Satisfaction: Guidelines for Monitoring and Measuring	**2012**
ISO 10005 Quality Management Systems: Guidelines for Quality Plans	**2005**
ISO 10006 Quality Management Systems: Guidelines for Quality Management in Projects	**2003**
ISO 10007 Quality Management Systems: Guidelines for Configuration Management	**2003**
ISO 10008 Quality Management: Customer Satisfaction: Guidelines for Business-to-Consumer Electronic Commerce Transactions	**2013**
ISO 10012 Measurement Management Systems: Requirements for Measurement Processes and Measuring Equipment	**2003**
ISO/TR 10013 Guidelines for Quality Management System Documentation	**2001**
ISO 10014 Quality Management: Guidelines for Realizing Financial and Economic Benefits	**2007**
ISO 10015 Quality Management: Guidelines for Training	**1999**
ISO/TR 10017 Guidance on Statistical Techniques for ISO 9001:2000	**2003**
ISO 10018 Quality Management: Guidelines on People Involvement and Competence	**2012**

Standard	Year Published
ISO 10019 Guidelines for the Selection of Quality Management System Consultants and Use of Their Services	**2005**
ISO 13485 Medical Devices: Quality Management Systems: Requirements for Regulatory Purposes	**2009**
ISO 14000 Environmental Management Systems: General Guidelines on Principles, Systems, and Supporting Techniques	**2015**
ISO 14969 Quality Systems: Medical Devices: Guidance on the Application of ISO 13485 and ISO 13488	**1999**
ISO 16106 Packaging Transport Packages for Dangerous Goods: Dangerous Goods Packaging, Intermediate Bulk Containers (IBCs), and Large Packaging Guidelines for the Application of ISO 9001	**2006**
ISO/TS 16949 Quality Management: Particular Requirements for the Application of ISO 9001:2008 for Automotive Production and Relevant Service Part Organizations	**2011**
ISO 15161 Guidelines on the Application of ISO 9001:2000 for the Food and Drink Industry	**2001**
ISO 15378 Primary Packaging Materials for Medicinal Products: Particular Requirements for the Application of ISO 9001:2008, with Reference to Good Manufacturing Practice (GMP)	**2011**
ISO 19011 Guidelines for Auditing Management Systems	**2011**

Standard	Year Published
ISO 16106 Packaging Transport Packages for Dangerous Goods: Dangerous Goods Packaging, Intermediate Bulk Containers (IBCs) and Large Packaging Guidelines for the Application of ISO 9001	**2006**
ISO 22000 Food Safety Management Other Systems Requirements for Any Organization in the Food Chain	**2005**
ISO/IEC 27000 Information Technology: Security Techniques: Information Security Management Systems: Overview and Vocabulary	**2014**
ISO/TS 29001 Petroleum, Petrochemical and Natural Gas Industries: Sector-Specific Quality Management Systems: Requirements for Product and Service Supply Organizations	**2010**
ISO 31000 Risk Management: Principles and Guidelines	**2009**
ISO 37500 Guidance on Outsourcing	**2014**
TL 9000 TL 9000 Quality Management System for Telecommunications	**2008**

C

Documentation

It is necessary to have reliable documentation to either control your work or to provide evidence that work was performed according to pre-established criteria and its results were based on original requirements. Documentation is also helpful for knowledge transfer and training of employees. There are other business reasons for documented information as well. For example, your employees may go on vacation and you may have to do their work and support other related activities in their absence. Often employees leave the company and you need to find a way to continue to do his or her work. Another obvious reason for keeping documentation relates to legal actions: The history of processes that are adhered to and related documented evidence will be required if litigation is filed. In any lawsuit, if you have to defend any adverse effect of your product or service, documented information will be essential in supporting your case.

In ISO 9001:2008, the terms "documented procedure" and "record" are used in the standard. In the revised ISO 9001:2015, these terms are replaced by a single term: "documented information." The need for *documented procedures* is now expressed as a requirement to *maintain* documented information, and the *records* previously mentioned in ISO 9001:2008 are now referred to as *retained* documented information. (Remember: "Documents are *maintained* while records are *retained*.)

Each organization can determine the type of documentation that is necessary to control its quality management system and to demonstrate that it is achieving intended results. The determination related to the extent of documentation can be made based on multiple criteria, such as the following:

- The size of the organization
- The type of activities, processes, services and or products
- The knowledge, expertise, and competence of employees
- The interactions between processes
- The complexity of processes

ISO 9001:2008 refers to documented procedures as a control or as information to support a process. This concept is now expressed as a requirement to maintain documented information. In ISO 9001:2015, *documented information* is defined as the information required to be controlled and maintained by an organization. The documented system includes any medium in which it is contained and defines the management system and related processes including documentation created so that the organization can operate efficiently with records (results or evidence) of achievement.

There are six clauses in ISO 9001:2015 where documented information is required to be maintained:

	Clause	Documented Information Requirement
1	4.3	Stating the scope of the QMS
2	4.4	The extent necessary to support operation of the organization processes
3	5.2.2a	Available for quality policy
4	7.5.1a	Required by this international standard
5	7.5.1b	Determined by the organization as necessary for the effectiveness of the QMS
6	7.5.3.2	Determined by the organization as necessary for the planning and operation of the QMS

As previously stated, the records required in ISO 9001:2008 are now documented information, which are required to be *retained*. We are highlighting the clauses that contain the requirement of retaining documented information:

	Clause	Documented Information Requirement
1	4.4	Necessary to have confidence that determined processes are adhered to
2	6.2.1	On the quality objectives
3	7.1.5	As evidence of fitness for the purpose of monitoring and measurement resources
4	7.1.5	On the basis used for calibration or verification where no such standards exist
5	7.2 d	As evidence of competence
6	7.5.1a	Required by this international standard
7	7.5.1b	Determined by the organization as being necessary for the effectiveness of the QMS

	Clause	Documented Information Requirement
8	8.1e	To the extent necessary to have confidence that the processes have been carried out as planned
9	8.1e	To demonstrate the conformity of products and services to their requirements
10	8.2.3	Of customer requirements
11	8.2.3	On the results of requirement review
12	8.3.2j	To demonstrate that design and development requirements have been met
13	8.3.5	On design and development outputs
14	8.3.6	On design and development changes
15	8.4.1	On the evaluation, selection, monitoring, or performance and reevaluation of external providers
16	8.5.1a	That defines the characteristics of products and services
17	8.5.1a	The results to be achieved
18	8.5.2	Necessary to enable traceability
19	8.5.6	Describing the results of the review of changes, the person authorizing the change, and the actions from the review
20	8.6	On evidence of conformity with the acceptance criteria; traceability to the person authorizing the release of a product or service
21	8.7	That describes nonconformity, actions taken, and concessions obtained; identifies the person who made the decision in addressing the nonconformity
22	9.1.1	As evidence of monitoring and measurement results
23	9.2.2f	As evidence of the implementation of the audit program and audit results
24	9.3.2	As evidence of the results of management reviews
25	10.2.2a	As evidence of the nature of nonconformities and actions taken
26	10.2.2b	As evidence of the results of any corrective actions

Maintained documented information may include items such as processes, test plans, pilot results, verification and validation results, customer requirements, process flow diagrams, and charts and checklists, among others. Note that ISO 9001:2015 takes a minimal approach to documentation (which has been a major revision). However, where documentation is intended to "retain" information, the purpose is show evidence of the organization's compliance with the standard and to indicate a certain activity was addressed and successfully accomplished for the smooth operation of the QMS.

D

Templates

Depending on the organization you represent, the extent and depth of each document discussed in this annex may differ. The intention here is simply to provide you with some guidance on the creation of these important policies, reports, and agendas. Feel free to customize these samples as you deem appropriate for your company and to change the contents to suit your needs and requirements.

Quality Policy

Establishing a quality policy provides strategic direction from top management to all employees regarding the company's goals and objectives; it also provides the entire company with a direction and an understanding of management's vision of quality. The quality policy must state the scope of the QMS and must state the responsibility to continually improve the effectiveness of the QMS. It must support the quality objectives as well. For example, if your quality policy states that you will "increase positive customer experiences," then you must focus on those activities that will help you to accomplish this aim—that is, the purchasing experiences of your customers, the customers' experiences with the implementation of your product or service, and the customers' experiences in obtaining customer support. For each of these activities, you must have related metrics that provide data that you can analyze and apply to improve less well-performing areas.

Each statement in your quality policy must be executable, meaning that everyone throughout the organization can understand it and is able to implement in his or her daily work. However, your top management must be involved in providing a clear direction for establishing and reviewing ongoing objectives and holding individuals accountable for the implementation of the objectives and associated measurements.

You must have a plan for how the quality policy will be communicated internally, thereby ensuring that the staff will understand it and will know what is expected of them. Periodically, the quality policy must be reviewed to ensure that it is still relevant. In an ever-changing business environment characterized by shifting customer needs and ongoing global/economic changes, the quality policy may require changes on a regular basis. In this case, the changes have to be communicated, new objectives developed, and people trained to maintain a smoothly running QMS.

Quality Policy: Example 1

John Doe & Company is committed to improving customer experience and ensuring that the customers have the best services from the company.

To realize this goal, the senior management and operations team of the company will regularly monitor pre-established metrics related to customer experiences, monitor the trends, and improve performance by continually implementing effective processes to enhance the customer experience.

Quality Policy: Example 2

John Doe & Company's management and employees are dedicated to providing quality products and services that continuously meet or exceed customer expectations. We are dedicated to continuous improvement of our quality management system to increase our productivity, improve our employee satisfaction, and improve our customer satisfaction.

Nonconformance Report

A nonconformance report captures the details of nonconformances that represent breaches of process adherence or the QMS standard, which perhaps were uncovered during an external or internal quality audit. The purpose of the report is to articulate clearly the problem so that corrective action can be taken to address the nonconformance. To confirm the nonconformance, whenever a nonconformance is found, it should be verified by an employee of the organization undergoing the audit. This will eliminate controversies about such issues that arise at a later time.

Template: Content of a Nonconformance Report

- **Date:** Date of the audit when the violation (noncompliance) was discovered
- **Auditee:** Name of the individual being audited
- **Location:** Physical location of the audit
- **Address:** Address of the organization or functional department being audited
- **Observation:** Give a statement of the noncompliance
- **Item:** The work item (e.g., process, plan, work item, policy) against which the violation occurred
- **Evidence:** List the evidence of the no-compliance (e.g., "Clause 8.6, Development Methodology, requires all test plans to be reviewed. No evidence was found in compliance with clause 8.6. The engineer audited stated that no reviews are conducted of the test plans.")

Nonconformance Report: Example

Date: August 26, XXXX

Auditee: John Doe

Location: McLean, Virginia 22101

Address: 1520 Mayflower Court

Observation: No evidence of review being conducted for ThinkPad Product, version III. Mr. Doe said that he was not aware of the procedure that required him to conduct a review of the test plan.

Item: Section 3.4 of the Development Methodology, Item 2a, states "All test plans, regardless of the size of the project, shall be reviewed and minutes of the review kept as a record."

Evidence: Mr. Doe's manager, Mr. George Brown, confirmed that he has been with the department for five months and have never seen a review of any product test plan conducted.

Internal Audit Report

An audit includes collecting evidence of procedures of an organization and their implementation to determine compliance with QMS requirements, and thereby the requirements of ISO 9001:2015. At the end of an audit, a report is developed by the lead auditor. The internal audit report contains critical information regarding your company's operation within the functional area that was audited.

Template: Internal Audit Report

Names of the Auditors: List the full name of each auditor

Date of the Audit: DD/MM/YYYY

Location of the Audit: Business unit audited (e.g., Maryland Business Unit, McLean Business Unit)

Areas Assessed: Functional organization audited (e.g., Engineering, Laboratory)

Individual (s) Audited: Names of individuals met during the audit

Scope: Specific areas to be audited

Objective and Results: List the objectives and observations

Observations and Action Plan: List of deficiencies, risks, and best practices (if appropriate). If no deficiencies (nonconformance) were observed, mention this in the report. Give action items expected from the auditee to close the deficiency.

Action Plan Person Responsible: Individual who is accountable to close the deficiency and estimated completion date

Signatures of the Auditors

Internal Audit Report: Example

Names of Auditors: Joe Blank and Marcie Brown

Location: Bethesda Branch

Areas Assessed: Accounts Payable

Individual Audited: Vicky Martino

Scope of the Audit:

- Accounts receivable at Bethesda Branch
- Payment processing activity for the past one year

Objectives and Results

The purpose of the audit was to evaluate process adherence to the pre-established procedures documented in the company's "accounts payable life cycle."

The objectives are listed below, along with the assessment categories: Satisfactory, Needs Improvement, Nonconformance.

Objectives	Control Assessment
Analyzing individual invoices	Satisfactory
Payment processing, including safeguarding of checks	Needs Improvement
Check authorizations and timely mailing	Unsatisfactory

Control Summary

Positives	Weak Controls
■ Invoices are checked thoroughly for the amount and items listed. ■ Checks are kept locked up at all times. ■ All processes listed in the APLC are adhered to, very closely.	■ Once checks are printed, they wait for two to three days for proper signatures due to unavailability of check signers. ■ Once the checks are signed, they are not mailed the same day, as required by the APLC. Evidence showed that on March 1, 2015, the checks remained in the office to be mailed for two days due to a work backlog. ■ Two new employees who are being trained indicated they did not have time to review and learn the APLC.

Observation and Action Plan

Listed on the next page are observations and related risk ratings.

Risk Ranking	MEDIUM

- There were no controls in place to ensure the checks were signed the same day they were printed as prescribed by procedure 7/1 of the APLC.
- The signed checks were not mailed the same day, as documented in procedure 8.1.1 of the APLC.
- New employees were not trained on the APLC and did not have time to review it, as prescribed by procedure 3.2 of the APLC.

Recommendation

- Ensure all A/P employees are trained and retrained on the APLC.
- Communicate to the employees the importance of process adherence.
- Make training of APLC part of new-employee orientation.
- Ensure the availability of check signers to eliminate the printed checks mailing delay.

Action Plan Responsibility

Person Responsible	John Doe	Estimated Completion Date	MM/DD/YY

Opening Meeting of an Audit

The opening meeting is initiated by the lead auditor; its purpose is to confirm the audit plan prior to beginning the audit. This meeting offers an opportunity to introduce the audit team members, discuss the approach of the audit, and answer any questions that come up related to the audit. A well-run, professional opening meeting sets the stage for the audit and creates mutual trust and an overall positive impression.

Consider some of the following elements when planning for the opening meeting:

- Your name, role, and QMS activities that you may be involved in
- Scope of the audit: for example, all activities of the Benefit Department of the Payroll organization
- Introduction of the attendees and clarification of the role of the guide
- Auditees: Individuals performing work within the scope of the audit
- Explain the closing meeting and what to expect in it

- Audit process: explanation of activities that will be addressed during the audit, such as the following:
  - One-on-one interviews with the individual performing the work
  - Evidence documents such as records
  - Review of process-related documents
  - Evidence of training
  - Evidence of verification and validation activities
- Methodology: details on the ratings of findings and observations:
  - Minor nonconformance: a minor deficiency in adhering to the organization's requirements or a single observation in one item of the organization's QMS
  - Major nonconformance: a major deficiency in adherence to the standard or the organization's pre-established QMS
  - Best practice observations: areas that have excelled in the implementation of a practice and have yielded exceptional results

Audit Interviews

To conduct successful audit interviews, certain skills are helpful. Interviews, reviews and examinations of documents, and visual observations are some of the verification methods. Other objective evidence may include items such as design drawings, checklists, pilot results, websites, and minutes of meetings.

Following are some recommended techniques for interviews:

- Ensure the interviewee is placed at ease and does not feel that he or she is being interrogated.
- Explain the purpose of the interview and why you will be taking notes so the individual does not feel threatened.
- Request that the interviewee to describe his or her job, activities related to the job, and processes used in the job.
- Use open-ended questions to encourage the individual to be open and provide additional information that may become pertinent to the audit.
- At the end, thank the interviewee and summarize the audit results.
- All audit findings should be recorded to be discussed during the closing meeting.

Daily Discussion Meetings

The daily discussion meetings during a multiple-day audit are usually held at the end of the day with management and the individuals audited during the day. These meetings are brief, lasting only 20 to 30 minutes. The purpose of the meeting is to discuss the findings of the day and encourage open dialogue.

Often, during these meetings, the auditee produces additional evidence of conformity to a certain finding, which the auditor may not have had a chance to discover earlier. These meetings are usually informal.

- Discuss the functional area that was audited during the day.
- Provide the information gathered from the individuals audited.
- Discuss all the observations, including nonconformance.
- Ask whether there is additional material the auditee may have skipped during the audit.
- Encourage questions from the attendees.
- At the end of the meeting, confirm all the nonconformances, which you will share again in the closing meeting.
- Express thanks and discuss the next day's audit agenda.

Closing Meeting

At the end of the audit, to prepare for the audit meeting, the audit team reviews the audit findings and audit evidence. The closing meetings are conducted to discuss the audit and the findings with the management staff of the company being audited. A systematic and controlled approach to the closing meeting ends the audit in a professional way.

Depending on the auditors, the contents of closing meeting may vary.

- Key leaders, managers, and individuals audited are welcome to attend the closing meeting.
- Confirm the audit is complete with respect to the audit scope and objectives, and express thanks to the company members.
- Discuss the scope of the audit and provide an overview of the audit.
- Highlight the areas to be audited.
- Discuss best practice observations.
- Share any minor nonconformances found, with details (e.g., "No evidence of review minutes for Benefit Project XXX, dated XXXXX, as per the company's Development Methodology, Chapter 5, clause 5.2).
- Discuss any major nonconformance, along with data on the person(s) audited, the date, the area of concern, and the actual nonconformance details.
- Explain the time frame for addressing major nonconformances and corrective actions.
- Record the attendance at the meeting.
- Relay the message that a formal audit report will be sent.
- Conclude the audit.

Index

total involvement of process improvement, 149–150

TQM (total quality management), 146–147

Total involvement of process improvement, 149–150

TQM (total quality management), 146–147

Training
auditors, 125–126
for new employees, 96–97
records of, 26
tracking with a white erase board, 33

U

Underperformance
identifying, 31–32
of registered organizations, 29

Upgrading to ISO 9001:2015, 20

User group meetings, 108

V

Validation, definition, 3–4

Value added perspective on improvements, 137–139

Value propositions, 77–78

Verification
definition, 3–4
of nonconformities, 134

Vision statements, reevaluating your QMS, 21–23

W

Wasteful activities. *See also specific activities.*
appraisal costs, 50
external failure, 50
internal failure, 48–49
prevention activities, 49–50
types of, 48–50. *See also specific types.*

WG (Work Group), 11

WG 23, 12

WG 24, 11, 34

White erase board, for tracking training, 33

WIFM (what's in it for me), 35–36